# CREATIVE GRANDPARENTING

# CREATIVE GRANDPARENTING

## HOW TO LOVE AND NURTURE
## A NEW GENERATION

## JERRY AND JUDY SCHREUR
### with granddaughter Erin Schreur

DISCOVERY HOUSE
PUBLISHERS®

*Creative Grandparenting: How to Love and Nurture a New Generation*

Discovery House is affiliated with RBC Ministries,
Grand Rapids, Michigan.

**Library of Congress Cataloging-in-Publication Data**

Schreur, Jerry, 1941-
    Creative grandparenting : how to love and nurture a new
generation / Jerry and Judy Schreur with Erin Schreur.
        p.  cm.
    Includes bibliographical references and index.
    ISBN 978-1-57293-488-7 (alk. paper)
    1. Grandparenting—Religious aspects—Christianity.  I. Schreur,
Judy.  II. Schreur, Erin.  III. Title.
    BV4528.5.S37  2011
    248.8'45—dc23                               2011032935

PRINTED IN THE UNITED STATES OF AMERICA

First printing in 2011

*Lauren, Erin, Elena, Jay, and Kendall:*
*This book is really all about you. Our lives are*
*richer and more meaningful because of you.*
*We are most blessed to be your grandparents.*
*We love you and thank God for you every day.*
*Jerry & Judy*

*Grandpa and Grandma:*
*Thank you for allowing me to work with you on this*
*book. You will always be my greatest teachers.*
*Erin*

# Contents

# Acknowledgments

We would like to thank Carol Holquist and Judith Markham for encouraging us to once again write about "creative grandparenting." Your faith in us and your excitement for the subject made this book possible. We also wish to thank Miranda Gardner, whose editing expertise gave life to our words and ideas. Miranda's enthusiastic involvement and interaction made the editing process an enjoyable experience. Finally, we would like to thank the grandparents who shared their lives with us. Thank you for being creative, involved grandparents and letting us share your stories and ideas in this book.

# Creative Grandparenting Is for You

Nineteen years ago I (Jerry) held my two-hour-old grand-daughter, Kendall, in the palm of my hand and silently offered a prayer of thanksgiving to God. I have never forgotten that day; its importance rivals that of my wedding day and the day my firstborn child came into the world. Arthur Kornhaber, researcher and writer, reminds us that there are three natural, life-transforming events in our lives over which we have no control: our birth, our death, and becoming grandparents. Even now, nineteen years later and with Kendall on her way to college, my heart skips a beat thinking about that moment when I held her in my hand.

I never dreamed, even then, that grandparenting would define my life quite like it has. Not a day goes by that I do not think about my five grandchildren, now ranging in age from nineteen to twenty-seven. Seldom does a week pass without me talking to or spending time with each one of them, even though they are scattered across the country, working and studying. Judy and I find—and make—time to be with them every chance we get. We are disappointed if we miss their calls; we cancel dinner plans with friends when our grandchildren come into town; we delay planning vacations until we know if we will be missing out on a chance to spend time with them. Vacations can be rescheduled and friends can wait, but being with our grandchildren cannot. There is simply no such thing as being with them enough. We are creative, involved grandparents. You can be too—there is no greater privilege.

## Creative Grandparents Described

Creative grandparents find new ways to love and enjoy their grandchildren at every age and stage of their lives. They know them intimately, what they are thinking and dreaming, their fears and struggles. They know when to talk and when to listen. They have the awesome privilege of watching their grandchildren become all they will be. This kind of close relationship imparts profound joy but also carries a weight and confers responsibility. In return for getting to be part of their lives, grandparents have a responsibility to be available, to be accepting, and to love unconditionally.

Being available is taking time out of your busy schedule to be with them. It means making them a priority, choosing to be with them instead of doing other things and being other places. It is fitting into their schedules, not demanding they fit into yours, or trying to squeeze them into your limited time. It is fulfilling your promises to them, being there when they count on you. Most importantly, it is letting them know how important they are to you and to God.

Loving and accepting your grandchildren unconditionally is seeing their uniqueness and the uniqueness of their individual journeys, not expecting them to be like you, their parents, or anyone else. It is looking for and encouraging their good qualities and positive traits, not focusing on negative traits. It is listening to their ideas and suggestions and doing what makes them happy when possible and practical. It is enjoying each one of them and letting them know how grateful you are for them and for the privilege of being a part of their lives.

Creative grandparents actively look for ways to be involved in the lives of their grandchildren, and enter their world, wherever and whenever allowed or invited. Creative grandparents know the interests and passions of their grandchildren and share their own with them. They are open to learning from their grandchildren and trying new things together. Creative grandparents are grateful for each opportunity to include them in their plans, but also allow them to say no to their invitations, without feeling personally rejected.

Creative grandparents enjoy their grandchildren, not merely endure them. Creative grandparents look into the eyes of their grandchildren, connect with them, see the love in their eyes, and respond to that love with a greater love. Creative grandparents walk with them, hand in hand through life, in good times and in tough times. Creative grandparents experience the great joy of having their grandchildren look up at them and say, "I just love to be with you, Grandpa." Creative grandparents thank God for their grandchildren and for their relationship with them each and every day, leading grandparents to wonder what they could possibly have done to be so privileged. Kornhaber and Woodward in *Grandparents/ Grandchildren* call this relationship "the vital connection . . . second only in emotional power to the parent-child bond."

Grandparenting is a unique and special joy. We can delight in the love and affection of our grandchildren without having to parent them. We can watch them grow into young men and women without having to keep track of curfew or worry about their school work. Grandparenting offers all the best things about parenting without the accompanying weight of responsibility. We can be free to enjoy our grandchildren in a way that we may not have been able to enjoy our children. We are older, seasoned, perhaps less rigid with the passing of years. We're more ready to laugh and cry, better prepared to love without reservation.

There are biological grandparents and there are creative grandparents. Biological grandparents carry pictures in their wallets and hang photos on the wall. They have sporadic contact with their grandchildren and limited input in their lives; they are gift-givers and perfunctory hug-receivers. Creative grandparents carry memories in their hearts and love in their souls. Creative grandparents go beyond showing off their grandchildren as trophies. They want to impart to them their values. Christian grandparents serve God and their grandchildren by teaching them about Jesus. They seek to live in a way that makes them heroes of faith to their grandchildren. They shower their grandchildren with love and acceptance. They build deep, meaningful relationships that will last a lifetime. Creative grandparents make a difference in the lives of their grandchildren.

This book is about creative grandparenting. Creative grandparenting goes beyond the occasional phone call and birthday present. It challenges to you to take grandparenting seriously. Judy and I want to help you realize that, as grandparents, we can have a profound influence on our grandchildren, and they on us. We want to inspire you to be the best creative grandparents you can be.

## The Benefits of Creative Grandparenting

The creative grandparenting challenge isn't something we take lightly or take on without reason. We believe that grandchildren benefit greatly from a strong relationship with their grandparents, and research has indicated this time and time again. Studies show heightened self-esteem, greater chance of success in later life, and a stronger sense of family values in adults who have had good relationships with their grandparents. The facts are in. They tell us that, now more than ever, children need love and acceptance. Now more than ever, children need trusted adults to tell them that they are okay. Now more than ever, children need role models, adults living out their faith and values with honesty and integrity.

As much as our grandchildren need us, we need our grandchildren. The benefits of being a creative, involved grandparent are many. When interviewing grandparents we constantly heard the phrase, "My grandchildren keep me young." They do. They show our tired bodies what it is like to run barefoot through the summer grass. They inspire us by scaling the trees we climbed in our youth. Their youthful enthusiasm reminds us of days long past. Grandchildren give us a renewed sense of what is possible. They give birth to new hope in us, reminding us of things we have forgotten about ourselves and teaching us things we've never known.

They also let us into the world of young people today. One grandmother we know listens to the music of her teenage grandson. She says, "I just want to know what's going on in the world, and John helps me stay in touch. He never treats me like an 'old fogey' but thinks it's kind of neat to lend me his CDs and create playlists for my iPod. He even brags to his friends that his grandma likes hip-hop." As we get older, we may begin to feel isolated from our families and from the mainstream of society. Our grandchildren bring us back. They provide us with an entrance into the world again, a ticket to American culture.

## Looking Ahead

In this book you will meet our five grandchildren—Lauren, Elena, Erin, Jay, and Kendall. You will hear their stories and memories and those of their parents, our sons, Jack and Jon. You will also hear stories from some of the hundreds of grandparents and grandchildren we have interviewed, counseled, or met over the years. Since the publication of the first edition of this book almost twenty years ago, a new voice has been added to Judy's and mine. The new voice is our granddaughter Erin, now all grown up and a writer and poet in her own right. She has written chapter 5, "On Their Own." (Judy and I ask your forgiveness if we come across as exceptionally proud and delighted with our grandkids—quite simply we are and it comes through in everything we do.)

*Creative Grandparenting* was written for every person who wants to make a difference in the lives of his or her grandchildren. This book is for grandparents who want to love their grandchildren with actions, not just words. Through *Creative Grandparenting* you will begin to see just how important a role we can play in the lives of our grandchildren, regardless of their age, or ours.

In this book you will read about grandparenting at every stage of your grandchildren's lives, from their early years to adulthood, and also in especially difficult times. You will discover new ways to connect with your grandchildren, despite "mountains, miles, and oceans" or even differences that separate you. You will be reminded of the importance of living in harmony with your own children, which is imperative if you are to be involved in your grandchildren's lives. You may have found already that parenting and grandparenting your grandchildren are very different tasks; we will suggest ways to successfully do both when necessary. Finally, you will be challenged to leave a lasting legacy to impact your grandchildren for eternity.

Most of all, we hope that *Creative Grandparenting* will inspire you to become a creative, involved grandparent. It is not always the easy road. With the joy and happiness we can also expect deep pain and disappointment. But, as the other grandparents you will meet in this book will testify, we guarantee that you will not regret your decision to become a creative grandparent. You will laugh as you have never laughed, hurt more deeply than you thought possible, and live with more vitality than ever before because you will be that most blessed of people, a creative grandparent.

# CHAPTER 1

# Our Many Roles

According to the AARP, today's 80 million grandparents in the United States are likely to be healthy, financially stable, and have a living spouse. These grandparents range in age from 30 to 110 with a median age of 55. They became grandparents in midlife, at an average age of 47. Many of these grandparents eagerly anticipated this stage of their lives and were well prepared for their first grandchild. Others were not excited. They saw the birth of their first grandchild as an unwelcome reminder of their own increasing age. Grandparenting is a responsibility to them, not a privilege. This is especially true for those who end up parenting their grandchildren.

It is within every grandparent's grasp to make grandparenting one of the best times of life. Grandparents make choices every day regarding their involvement with their grandchildren. Some will let the time slip away and pursue their own interests during their grandchildren's formative years. Creative grandparents will actively look for ways to become involved in the lives of their grandchildren, at every age and stage of their grandchildren's lives.

Creative grandparents play many roles in the lives of their grandchildren: historian, mentor, role model, nurturer, and hero. What does it take to play these roles well? Creative grandparents must be defined by the qualities of readiness, selflessness, passion, openness, flexibility, understanding, acceptance, and availability. These qualities help to insure success in the many important roles grandparents play in their grandchildren's lives.

## The Qualities That Must Define Us

Creative grandparents impact their grandchildren in so many ways through the roles they play in their lives, which is why grandparents must develop qualities that enable them to become involved, effective grandparents.

### Readiness

Soon-to-be creative grandparents often express an eagerness to become grandparents. They are ready for their upcoming role and excited about this new stage of life. Many of them admit they "can't wait to become grandparents." They look forward to the birth of their first grandchild and every grandchild thereafter with an excitement seldom matched by any other event, and it's easy to see why. When they hold that child in their arms for the first time, new energy, vitality, and purpose take hold of them. They know their lives will be forever different because of that child.

In the days and weeks to come, their steps seem lighter and their smile is more evident. They are more contented and fulfilled. They light up when they talk about their grandchildren. They are proud grandparents who are excited about dedicating the days ahead to their precious grandchildren. These creative grandparents are ready to devote their lives to loving and nurturing a new generation.

## Selflessness

Creative grandparents demonstrate a seemingly selfless devotion to their grandchildren. They are willing to forego time with friends and relatives or change personal plans to be with their grandkids. Researcher Joy Goodfellow describes this devotion and selflessness as "intergenerational altruism." This devotion is sometimes misunderstood, especially by those who do not have children or grandchildren. Friends and relatives may not understand why grandparents would cancel plans with them to instead be with their grandchildren when they come into town, and they may even consider grandparents rude. Creative grandparents will not see their actions as rude, but as taking the opportunity to be with people more important to them than anyone else in the world—their grandchildren.

Creative grandparents willingly give up what they desire and value highly for something which is, for them, far better—being with their grandkids. They may even refuse a job promotion or turn down career advancement opportunities that require them to move a great distance away from their grandkids. Early in my pastoral ministry, I had an exciting opportunity to join a church staff in a part of the country that has something that Michigan does not: 14,000-foot mountains.

A friend invited me to join him on the staff of a large, growing church with opportunity for me to use my experience, education, and passion to develop a family ministry for their church. The church was one hour's drive from mountains and ski resorts. He knew that downhill skiing was one of my favorite sports and was surprised when I immediately responded with a firm, "No, I won't even think about it." My friend could not understand why I had turned down the job and asked me to reconsider and pray about the decision. I told him that I would not entertain the thought of moving away from my five grandchildren, no matter how attractive the offer. Then he understood.

I knew that someday my grandkids would attend college, move away from me, and eventually start their own careers, possibly in other parts of the country or world. But at the time they were with me, an integral part of my life, and I of theirs. I would not change that for career opportunities or mountains with ski resorts. Two years later I met the person who took that job. He shared with me how the church had grown substantially and that it was a wonderful place for family ministry, the best job he had ever held. Still, that decision was, and is, a no-brainer. Any opportunity that would take me away from my grandchildren would not be considered, not even for a minute. Now, more than fifteen years later, I have no regrets. Instead, I have had fifteen more years of enjoying and loving my grandchildren. As my grandchildren matured and that story was related to them, they understood in yet another way their grandfather's love and devotion to them.

My decision to stay was confirmed a few years later, when another grandfather, a friend of mine, moved a thousand miles away from his grandchildren for a job, and then promptly moved back to Michigan. When I saw him, I asked what he was doing back after only three months away. With tears in his eyes he said to me, "Jerry, we made a terrible mistake moving away from our grandchildren. We missed them so much we had no choice but to move back to be close to them again. We are so much happier now. The job doesn't matter. Being with our grandkids does. We made the right choice, to move back. I don't know what got into me, to move away from my grandkids. I guess I just wasn't thinking clearly."

### Passion

Creative grandparents possess a passion for life that is contagious, a positive attitude about life itself, and gratitude for each day God has given them to enjoy, especially the days they get to spend with their grandchildren. That passion helps them to enthusiastically embrace each day with their grandchildren as another "day the Lord has made" (Psalm 118:24). This passion creates the energy and vitality necessary for grandparents to keep up with energetic, active, growing grandchildren, who often will tax grandparents' strength and stamina. Creative grandparents' passion also creates wonder and awe in their grandchildren, which inspires and challenges grandchildren to experience life more fully and enjoy each day that God gives them.

### Openness

Creative grandparents must be open to new experiences, willing to try new things at every age and stage of their grandkids' lives. We did not grown up in the world of our grandchildren, and therefore have not had opportunities to do many of the things our grandchildren love. Some grandparents may be apprehensive about trying new things, especially at their age. The tendency might be to negatively respond to a suggestion by grandchildren to participate in something new, especially if it creates fear and anxiety. Creative grandparents overcome their fear, dive in, and join their grandkids, doing things they never dreamed of doing when they were kids. They face new challenges in order to be with their grandkids and enjoy the experiences of life together.

The new activities become learning experiences, stretching grandparents and expanding their lives. Lillian Carson, in her book *The Essential Grandparent*, says it well: "Grandchildren provide an avenue that leads us right into life. With them we experience life unfolding. Their fresh view not only delights us but awakens us to new possibilities. It's refreshing. It's healthy. It keeps us young. It is the joy of grandparenting."

As I write these words, my twenty-two-year-old grandson, Jay, and I are planning to skydive together with his two sisters this spring. Even though I was a bit apprehensive, which is probably true for most sixty-plus-year-old grandparents, I finally said, "Let's do it." Jay has already jumped once, in New Zeeland, and assures me it is really quite safe, as we will be jumping tandem, with instructors. By the time you read these words this event will be part of our family history, another exciting life event shared with our grandchildren. Grandmother Judy will probably come along for the ride, but will not jump. However, I can assure you she will pray, and all of us will appreciate that.

*Flexibility*

Creative grandparents must be flexible, not rigid with their grandchildren. This flexibility lets grandparents adapt to changing situations and be patient with grandchildren who may be different from them and different from each other. Sometimes one or more of our grandkids will say no to our suggestions, because they are not interested. It is okay if our grandchildren choose not to participate in some events. It is not personal rejection, but rather personal choice and preferred interests. We need to be flexible and creative with suggestions for spending time with our grandchildren.

*Understanding*

Creative grandparents possess an atypical desire to understand their grandchildren. They want to understand their uniqueness, their interests, and their problems so they can connect with and enjoy them. They ask a lot of questions, not because they are nosy, but because they want to know their grandkids intimately. They want to know what is happening in their lives. They want to celebrate their successes and encourage them when they struggle or fail. They want to meet their needs whenever possible and practical. They even want to meet their friends and understand them too. Understanding our grandchildren leads to acceptance.

*Acceptance*

Creative grandparents genuinely accept their grandchildren for who they are, appreciate their individuality, and love them as unique, wonderful creations of God. They celebrate their uniqueness instead of criticizing them for their differences. Each one of my five grandchildren has different interests, abilities, needs, and sensitivities. Yet we accept and enjoy each grandchild. We share our passions and celebrate our differences, and say with the psalmist,

> I praise you because I am fearfully and wonderfully made; your works are wonderful, I know that full well. My frame was not hidden from you when I was made in the secret place. When I was woven together in the depths of the earth, your eyes saw my unformed body. All the days ordained for me were written in your book before one of them came to be. How precious to me are your thoughts, O God! (Psalm 139:14–17 NIV)

One of our granddaughters seems to be attracted to artistic men who love music. We love music but not always the kind her friends play. However, her friends are our friends and we accept them with their music and unconventional hairstyles because we love our granddaughter. We are grateful for the unique way in which God has created us, praise God for each one of our grandchildren, and celebrate their differences.

### *Availability*

Creative grandparents want to be with their grandchildren. They make themselves available. Their calendar is filled with appointments with their grandchildren. Presence is what they crave. They look for excuses to see them. They travel hundreds of miles just to be with them. They find the money necessary for those visits, sometimes foregoing other opportunities with friends and family. They volunteer to provide child-care when parents need help. They say yes more than no. Spending time with their grandchildren takes priority over almost everything else in their life.

A good friend called me recently and wanted to get together for dinner. We had not seen each other for a couple of months and were looking forward to getting together again, as soon as possible. As we talked on the phone and looked at our calendars for times to meet for dinner, I had to decline the first two suggestions because of prior commitments to my grandchildren. When I told my friend that those dates would not work, that they were already taken by my grandkids, he kidded me about not wanting to be with him, but I knew that he was only kidding, because he too is a creative grandparent who takes every opportunity to be with his grandchildren.

Creative grandparents have a mutual understanding when it comes to opportunities to be with their grandchildren. Grandchildren are always first—that's just the way it is, nonnegotiable. When grandparents possess these qualities, they are ready to play important roles in the lives of their grandchildren.

## Our Many Roles

Creative grandparents play several roles throughout the lives of their grandchildren. They are historians, mentors, models, nurturers, and heroes. All of these roles are significant and important as grandparents seek to love and nurture a new generation.

### Historian

Arthur Kornhaber calls grandparents "living time machines that transport children to the past through first-hand accounts of family history." As historians, grandparents tell their family story, giving grandchildren a sense of the past and creating awareness of family roots. They tell stories of themselves, their parents, and their grandparents. Some of the stories are funny, some serious, some insightful. One grandmother was telling her little granddaughter what her own childhood was like: "We used to skate outside on a pond. I had a swing made from a tire; it hung from a tree in our front yard. We rode our pony. We picked wild raspberries in the woods." The wide-eyed girl said, "I sure wish I'd gotten to know you sooner!"

Storytelling gives us a sense of history and connection. One storyteller for *Joy!* magazine put it this way:

> Not only are stories fun, but they also kindle interest, spark creativity, convey wisdom, and impart values. God Himself is the supreme storyteller. When He wanted to reveal Himself to us, He chose stories as His preferred way. Almost 70 percent of the Bible takes the form of stories. Both in the Bible and in the cultures of the world, stories have always been the preferred method of transferring values. The elders of Israel were master storytellers, educating their children with tales of great events of their past to give them a sense of their history and their destiny.

God instructed Joshua to tell future generations about His deliverance of the children of Israel from Egypt and their passing through the Jordan River on dry ground, into the Promised Land:

> When the whole nation had finished crossing the Jordan, the Lord said to Joshua, "Choose twelve men from among the people, one from each tribe, and tell them

to take up twelve stones from the middle of the Jordan from right where the priests stood and to carry them over with you and put them down at the place where you stay tonight . . . In the future, when your children ask you, 'What do these stones mean?' tell them that the flow of the Jordan was cut off before the ark of the covenant of the Lord. When it crossed the Jordan, the waters of the Jordan were cut off." (Joshua 4:1–3, 6–7 NIV)

I can picture a Jewish grandfather telling this story, with his grandchildren sitting in awe at his feet, asking questions like, "What happened then, Grandfather?" This grandfather would tell them about how their ancestors crossed the Jordan River on dry ground with walls of water on either side. He would tell them about the waters closing up after them. He would tell them of God's wonderful love and redemption of His people, Israel. The grandfather would then tell his grandchildren of his own love for God, and challenge them to love Him with all their heart, soul, and mind.

Creative grandparents are connectors to the past and to past generations. As Kornhaber says, "Grandparenting is the glue that bonds the generations." Grandparents provide connection between at least five generations: they are the third generation, their parents the fourth, and their grandparents the fifth generation. Our world has changed so dramatically in the last fifty to one hundred years. Our own grandparents experienced life in different ways than our grandchildren are experiencing it today. Those were the days without sports cars, without major highways, without television, without computers, and without Internet. Theirs was a world of scarcity, of war. Our grandchildren will find it hard to understand the world of our parents and grandparents unless we tell stories, unless we provide connections to the past.

Our stories give grandchildren a sense of connection to past generations and provide awareness of family roots, which in turn provide security and strength. These family roots help them shape an identity in a world increasingly rootless and difficult to navigate. We connect them to a tradition and a history that give them a place in the world.

### *Mentor*

Creative grandparents are also mentors to their grandchildren. Most grandparents have unique abilities and knowledge to share with their grandchildren. They know how to do things their grandchildren can't do (at least without some training and supervision). Creative grandparents are not only open to teaching their grandchildren these skills, they are also enthusiastic and willing to take the time necessary to share their knowledge and expertise with their grandchildren. One grandson said, "Grandpa is the smartest man on earth! He teaches me good things, but I don't get to see him enough to get as smart as him!"

My grandson, Jay, calls me at least once a month to help him fix his old Jeep, which always seems to have something wrong with it. Jay and I have replaced his muffler and tailpipe, repaired a lock on his door, and replaced his brakes on the front of his Jeep. More recently we repaired the rear brakes. After replacing the rear brake shoes and cylinders, and then bleeding the brake lines, we still had fluid leaking from one of the wheel cylinders. Whenever Jay and I work on his car, I usually share the job with him. I teach and supervise and usually allow him to do more than half of the work. With the brake jobs, Jay repaired one side and I repaired the other. He did the driver's side while I replaced the passenger side. When we checked the repairs to see what had gone wrong, Jay reminded me that it was my side that had been incorrectly repaired, causing brake fluid to leak from the cylinder. We agreed that my usual practice of checking Jay's work needed to be changed. From now on, Jay would check my work. We laughed together, fixed it correctly, and drove away, not only having fixed his car, but more importantly, having learned together and laughed together over Grandpa's mistake. Every grandparent has unique opportunities to mentor their grandchildren, to teach them something interesting or useful, for now and for later.

### Role Model

Creative grandparents are not only historians and mentors, but also role models for their grandchildren. Grandchildren often look beyond their parents to their grandparents for how life is to be lived—what to include and what to exclude, what to hold tightly and what to hold loosely. Sometimes children look up to grandparents because parents are not worthy role models. Some parents live their lives selfishly without regard for God and others. Others are not present in their children's lives because of work obligations, sickness, or incarceration. When these situations occur, children look to others for guidance and a path to follow. They need someone who will not only tell them the way to live and love, but also model that message with a godly life. Creative grandparents need to be able to say with the apostle Paul, "Follow my example, as I follow the example of Christ" (1 Corinthians 11:1 NIV).

Creative grandparents model morals, gender, and values. Grandparents teach the young social morality and give them a sense of right and wrong, a set of absolutes upon which they can build their lives. In this day of relative truth, grandchildren need models of truth and biblical morality, models that don't change with the times. They need to see integrity consistently displayed. Creative, involved grandparents provide grandchildren a model of morality to emulate.

Creative grandparents also model gender. This is why it is so important for grandfathers as well as grandmothers to be creatively involved in the lives of their grandchildren. Often grandmothers love and nurture grandchildren, but grandfathers need to be equally involved. Our grandsons must see a "man who does not walk in the counsel of the wicked or stand in the way of sinners." They need to see a man whose "delight is in the law of the Lord" (Psalm 1:1 NIV). They need to see "the man of integrity [who] walks securely" (Proverbs 10:9 NIV). Our grandsons must see men who respect their wives (1 Peter 3:7) and love them sacrificially "as Christ loved the church and gave himself up for her" (Ephesians 5:25 NIV). Now, more than ever before, our grandsons need a male role model who will be the man God intended him to be, a man after God's own heart. That is God's mandate for us as grandfathers.

Our granddaughters must see a woman of "noble character," a woman who "opens her arms to the poor," a woman who "fears the Lord," a woman whose "children arise to call her blessed" (Proverbs 31:10, 20, 28, 29 NIV). They must see a woman who is secure, a woman who is comfortable in her own skin. They must see a woman who treats her husband with respect (Ephesians 5:33), a woman with the "unfading beauty of a gentle and quiet spirit, which is of great worth in God's sight" (1 Peter 3:4 NIV). This is God's mandate for grandmothers who love God and desire to be creatively involved in the lives of their granddaughters.

Creative grandparents also model values, showing their grandchildren by their lives what is important and what is not important. Our verbalized values are meaningless to others, but lived-out values confirm our beliefs. James says, "I will show you my faith by what I do" (James 2:18 NIV). When grandparents freely give to their church or favorite charity and are unselfish with others, they model generosity for their grandchildren. When they are stingy and drop a dollar in the offering plate, that too is seen by little eyes. Grandparents' actions present a strong message to thoughtful grandchildren who are always watching. When grandparents willingly give of themselves to serve God and others and reach out to those in need, grandchildren see altruistic, unselfish people who "look not only to [their] own interests, but also to the interests of others" (Philippians 2:4 NIV). When we invite our grandchildren into our lives, they *may* listen to our words, but be assured, they *will* observe our works.

Several years ago a missionary friend invited me to go to Thailand. This was immediately after the tsunami that had wiped out the homes and businesses of thousands of Thai people, killed tens of thousands, and totally destroyed their economy. Whenever I have opportunities for new experiences, whether for ministry or recreation, I usually check with my grandkids to see who is available to share my experience. My granddaughter Erin was about to graduate from high school, with three weeks of classes remaining when I called her. She is my adventure girl, so I wasn't too surprised when she immediately responded, "Let's go, Grandpa." She checked with her high school principal and was encouraged to skip the last three weeks of school to help in a country where tens of thousands of people had died in one of the worst disasters of modern times. We got our required medical shots, purchased plane tickets, and flew halfway around the world, to Thailand.

The small village on the coast where we stayed had lost more than five thousand people, with many of them still missing. The sea had swallowed up entire families—washed them away—with recovery of some bodies impossible. People were devastated; tourism was nonexistent. Most hotels and resorts had been totally destroyed. There were piles of rubble everywhere. People wandered around listless, without purpose or meaning. While we were there some relatives of the missing came through our village, looking for loved ones. They showed us pictures and asked, "Have you seen my son?" or "Have you seen my daughter?"

Almost everyone we met had a story of tragedy and loss. A young lady in a Bible study we attended showed us a picture of her ten-year-old son, whose body had been found in a tree. He had climbed the tree in an effort to escape the thirty-three-foot waves. We cried together as we tried to comfort this young mother, still in mourning, who had become a Christian after her son's tragic death. Another young man survived by climbing a tree and hanging on tightly, but his eight friends all died. Erin and I spent three weeks listening to stories of loss, viewing the results of the disaster, and serving whenever and wherever we could.

Toward the end of our trip, we visited an orphanage for children infected with HIV in northern Thailand. We prayed with a mother who was dying of AIDS and held those beautiful Thai children in our arms. I will never forget watching Erin walk hand in hand with a small child, taking her back to the other children to play. I remember Erin's struggle as she left that orphanage. She strongly entertained the thought of staying in Thailand to serve God and the children in this orphanage. I think she would have stayed had I not firmly told her we needed to go home.

I remember asking a nurse why she was there, giving her life to serve these HIV-infected children and some mothers who were dying of AIDS. First she quoted Jesus' words:

> "For I was hungry and you gave me something to eat, I was thirsty and you gave me something to drink, I was a stranger and you invited me in, I needed clothes and you clothed me, I was sick and you looked after me, I was in prison and you came to visit me." Then the righteous will answer him, "Lord, when did we see you hungry and feed you, or thirsty and give you something to drink? When did we see you a stranger and invite you in, or needing clothes and clothe you? When did we see you sick or in prison and go to visit you?" The King will reply, "I tell you the truth, whatever you did for one of the least of these brothers of mine, you did for me." (Matthew 25:35–40 NIV)

She then turned to me and concluded with words that I will never forget: "These are the least of these of whom Jesus spoke." I walked away with those words in my heart and mind, trying to hide the tears in my eyes, with Erin at my side. The nurse saw that I was struggling, came over, gave me a hug, and asked me if I was okay. I said yes, but my life would never be okay again. After we arrived back home, Erin told me how her experience in Thailand had changed her life forever and that she too, would never be the same again.

We can spend our lifetime telling others how to live and how to love, often without much success. Better to let others, especially our grandchildren, observe a life devoted to God and serving others. Better yet, let them participate in your life and ministry to others, personally experiencing events that will challenge them and change their lives forever.

### Nurturer

Creative grandparents desire to nurture their grand-children, to see them grow up to become healthy, well-functioning, mature adults. To this task, grandparents give their time and energy. Creative grandparents serve as a backup system for parents and expand a child's support system. Having a grandparent who is always there brings security to a grandchild's life. One eighty-eight-year-old grandmother says, "I hope that my grandson has a feeling of security that I am here. If he has any needs, I hope that he will tell me about them. I want him to come and ask me if there is anything I can do for him." A grandparent's availability and willingness to help is particularly imperative in difficult times, or times in which children are estranged or separated from parents. Sometimes children just need another safe person to talk to, who will listen without judgment or criticism.

I remember counseling a young man for personal issues he was facing. He was making significant progress. But I wonder how much I helped this young man. One day he shared with me what was really happening in his life to help him grow in his faith. Every week after leaving my office, he would stop to see his grandfather for support and encouragement. He shared with me how his grandfather was a source of encouragement to him and how he could not wait to see him every week. I really believe that his grandfather helped him more than this experienced pastoral counselor who has many letters behind his name. Grandparents can sometimes do what trained, experienced counselors cannot. They should never underestimate their powerful influence on their grandchildren.

Grandparents encourage, build up, and nurture a new generation. They are there for their grandchildren when needed. One twenty-two-year-old granddaughter told us, "Grandparents are supposed to be there when you need them, and they always are. They're always there and they always have time for you. They're willing, able, ready—always." A sixty-eight-year-old grandmother stated, "Just to be there for them. If something is wrong, they can always feel free to come to you." Creative grandparents nurture their grandchildren.

### Hero

Creative grandparents are heroes to their grandchildren. Frank Farley, from the University of Wisconsin–Madison, surveyed 1,023 children ages ten to thirteen, and found that 43 percent of them had no role model or hero in their lives. Farley said, "Children's lack of heroes reflects a negativism in society and points out the need for more positive role models . . . It's very hard to teach people in the abstract about some complicated ideal. If you can show how that ideal is embodied in a person's life, it becomes clearer . . . Heroes tend to be unambiguous. They present a clear example." Heroes are characterized by courage, honesty, bravery, selflessness, and the will to try. Heroes don't give up easily. Heroes are people we admire and respect, people we look up to, and people who are dependable, consistent, and trustworthy.

Arthur Kornhaber, in his book *Grandparent Power*, expresses his concern for the lack of heroes for our children today: "In this era of fallen idols, when we no longer have heroic examples as heads of state, . . . and when the tabloids exploit every lurid detail of the lives of people in the public eye, your grandchildren need you as someone to look up to." Every grandson or granddaughter needs a hero. Grandparents, with God's help, can fill this vital role.

Our grandchildren need historians, mentors, models, nurturers, and heroes in their lives. Creative grandparents seem to be uniquely equipped to play these roles as they invite their grandchildren into their lives and enter into the lives of their grandchildren. Creative grandparents practice loving and nurturing this new generation at every age and stage of their lives, from the wonder years until the time they are on their own as healthy, well-functioning adults.

# CHAPTER 2

# The Wonder Years

The sailor-adventurers who set out from Europe on voyages of discovery hundreds of years ago were entering the unknown. They were going where they believed no one had ever been before. They were a superstitious lot, seeing the instability of wind and water as a result of the whims of capricious and resentful gods. The uncertainty of their destination and the unknown terrors that might await them inspired a deep longing for the safety of familiar waters and welcoming harbors.

Imagine a world like that. A world where all the mysteries we adults figured out long ago are still unfathomable perplexities. Imagine a world where every new noise inspires curiosity or fear; where every new form requires investigation and understanding. This is the world of your preschool grandchildren. Like sailors of old, they too are setting off on a daring voyage of discovery. They too, long for the safety of familiar waters even as they take their first tottering steps toward independence.

Grandma and Grandpa can serve as guides through these years of wonder. They can help grandchildren explore and learn how to feel at home amid the beauty and excitement of their new world. They can also be harbors of refuge when that world turns hostile and the young explorers' fears become overwhelming.

## Getting Started

He wasn't comfortable when he first held her. She was tiny and wrinkled; his hands were big and awkward. He felt a little foolish and even fearful. He thought he might crush her. He held her gingerly against his broad chest, so softly that he could scarcely feel her little heart beating against his own. He caught the scent of her breath, smelling ever so slightly of Elmer's glue. His heart was gone! His two-day-old granddaughter had stolen it.

The first year of life is crucial for children to gain a sense of trust that will outweigh their mistrust, according to child psychologist and author Erik Erikson. Studies show conclusively that caregivers who don't interact with their babies foster mistrust in them. The duty and joy of creative grandparenting is to be, along with the parents, caregivers who build trust.

Sometimes grandparents, especially grandfathers, are more frightened than the babies themselves of their new relationships and roles. That's because babies do the unexpected when Grandma and Grandpa babysit them. For instance, I never got used to holding my granddaughter or grandson when their eyes squeezed shut, their faces turned red, and their diapered bottoms rumbled in my hands and turned warm. I knew what was ahead—and behind. As any grandfather would, I ignored it as long as possible, until the state-of-the-art, high-tech, space-age diaper began to leak.

But creative grandparents don't let rumbling bottoms faze them. They take this opportunity to express their love and build trust with their grandchildren. All the while they carry on a one-sided conversation. "Kendall, you have a dirty, smelly diaper. Yes, you do. Oh yes, you do. Let's get that diaper off. Oh, you are so beautiful, so special. Grandpa loves you, even if you are stinky. Yes, he does. Yes, he does."

Not the most literate of conversations, but important. Constantly reassuring your grandchildren strengthens their trust in you—and in themselves. Diaper changing and baby talk may appear to be beneath your dignity after a lifetime in an office or courtroom or classroom, but creative grandparents must seize every opportunity to express their love.

## Grandparenting during Infancy

Understanding three simple keys to grandparenting infants will make this time a rewarding and joyful experience. The first key is to be available. New parents need help. A lot of it. It has been said often and truthfully that babies don't come with instructions. Especially if this grandchild is a first child, your children are going to be proud, excited, scared, worried, and overwhelmed, all at the same time. Parents need grandparents who are available to help with the multitude of chores during the baby's first year. Seemingly mundane tasks such as laundry, cooking, and shopping can be difficult to accomplish as parents juggle schedules, work, and a young child. Grandparents who are committed to creatively becoming a part of their grandchildren's lives will make themselves available to meet all kind of needs.

The second key to grandparenting during infancy is to stay in the background. How many times have we seen grandparents who desire to "help the new mother out" but instead exasperate parents by being bossy and domineering. "Here, put a sweater on that baby," "Where is his hat?" "You're not going to pick him up just because he is crying are you?" or, two of my favorites, "When you were a baby I would never have dressed you like that," and "You don't want my advice? Well remember, I've had a little more experience than you!" Grandparents who want to be available also need to stay out of the way, in the background, which is not always easy to do.

The third key to grandparenting babies is simple yet probably the most important of all—enjoy the wonder. Take time to be with your new grandchild; just hold him or her and allow yourself to feel the love and joy this little life brings. Take time to enjoy the wonder of babies.

Grandparenting during infancy is exciting. We get to share in the special joy of new life first becoming aware of the world. We do this by being available. We help our children creatively by babysitting and doing the little things we can. We grandparent well by staying in the background. No unsolicited advice, no guilt or manipulation, just affirmation and quiet love. We grandparent infants by celebrating their wonder. There is absolutely nothing so awesome as new life coming into the world. Shake yourself free from your duties, release your mind from your concerns and worries, and revel in the joy and unexpected pleasures of your infant grandchildren.

## The Preschool Years

The years that follow infancy will be exhilarating. These little bundles soon turn into dynamos of constant motion. Not a glance do they toss behind to see what they might have missed as they rush to learn and grow. These tiny persons awaken in their grandparents a profound sense of astonishment; they fill our lives with surprise.

These preschool years are wonder years—both for the children and their grandparents. Both are discovering the world. The children are seeing it for the first time. Their grandparents are seeing it anew, as if for the first time, through the eyes of their grandchildren.

Creative grandparenting during these wonder years is a joyful, life-affirming experience. Perhaps at no other time are grandchildren so open to their grandparents, so eager to trust, so willing to be kissed, hugged, and loved. Child psychologist David Elkind writes about these years in his book *Grandparenting*:

> Preschool children seem to show a particular affinity for grandparents. Perhaps they sense a maturity and stability that is only partial in parents who are still trying to sort out parenting, marriage, and career roles. Because young children are experiencing so much that is new, it is reassuring and comforting to them to have adults who are at ease with themselves and their world. With such adults they can feel free to explore their environment. They can try out new words and activities with a sense that the world is secure and that their explorations will be understood as just that—explorations, not mischief. Grandparents walk a fine line with these intrepid

little adventurers. In full support and cooperation with parents, Grandma and Grandpa can help them venture out and explore the sometimes harsh ways of the world. We can also be lighthouses, calling our venturesome grandchildren back to safety. We have to let them learn, sometimes through painful failure, and keep them from becoming discouraged. We encourage them to overcome their fears, while we understand that fears are reasonable for a tiny child in a vast, mysterious world.

## Communicating Love

Four-year-old Kate bounded into the house. Grandma was on the phone with a friend. "Grandma, quick! I need to show you something."

"Shh, just a minute, Kate. I'm on the phone." Kate turned a couple of pirouettes, looked at Grandma, and said louder, "Gram, please! We have to hurry!"

"Kate, I'm almost done. Be patient." Grandma Ruth could not conceal a little smile. Kate was fairly bursting. Ruth quickly ended her conversation and said, "Okay, Kate, what's the big emergency?"

"Grandma, follow me! Quick!" Kate ran down the hall and out the door. Ruth came as fast as she could, wishing she had the energy and vitality of her four-year-old granddaughter. She followed Kate down the path to the barn. Kate ran to the far corner of the barn. "Look, Gram, look! They're babies! They were just born." Ruth looked into the shadowed corner and saw four squirming little kittens with their eyes still closed. They watched in silence as the mother nuzzled and groomed her babies. Kate and Ruth spontaneously reached out for each other and held hands. Kate looked up at her grandma and saw tears streaking her face. "What's wrong Grandma? Why are you crying?"

"I was just thinking about the day you were born. You were so tiny, but your lungs were so powerful. How you cried when you were hungry. You had lots of dark hair and bright pink cheeks. I was the proudest grandma in the whole world. I thought that you were the most beautiful child who had ever lived. I held you that first day while your mommy rested, and I fell in love with you. Watching these baby kittens in their first hours of life, seeing how happy they make you, makes me feel so close to you, sweetie. Thanks for insisting that I come with you. I love you so much."

As children grow, their ability to communicate grows with them. Each phase gives their grandparents fresh opportunities to express their love. It also challenges grandparents to acquire the skills of a linguist as they try to comprehend their grandchildren's undeveloped verbal expressions. One-sided conversations gradually become punctuated with an occasional, treasured "gub-oo-bampa."

Talks with grandchildren can be a nearly continuous stream of love. This does not mean that we need to say "I love you" three hundred times a day. Rather, the language should be open and inviting, the tone reassuring, the manner loving. Grandchildren should be able to feel the fire of love that burns in their grandparents' hearts. It should be apparent while Grandma is rocking one to sleep, or while Grandpa is cleaning out the garage with his two-year-old granddaughter's capable assistance.

Love-communication is not limited to speech. Nonverbal signals are equally important. A study by Albert Mehrabian revealed that about 7 percent of the message is delivered by the actual words. Tone of voice conveys 38 percent and nonverbal signals account for 55 percent of what we communicate. Even with very young grandchildren, *what* we say pales in importance compared with *how* we communicate, both verbally and nonverbally.

Creative grandparents know the value of a hug, a firm grip on the shoulder, an affectionate head-pat. One grandfather we know is particularly appreciated for his hugs. They are generous and abundant: very tight, very long, and his grandchildren love them. He wants them to get the idea that he will love them forever, no matter what. And while he holds his preschool grandchildren tightly, he gives them a steady stream of verbal affirmation. With words and actions, he is speaking volumes.

How do grandparents make the most of these precious years? How does Grandma or Grandpa give those little explorer-adventurers what they need most from them? We'd like to offer eight tips for creative grandparents of two- to five-year-olds.

## Tip #1: Love Your Grandchildren All-ways

Grandparents cannot express their love too much, too often, or in too many ways to their wonder-years grandchildren. We are not spoiling them when we give them constant reassurances of our love. On the contrary, we will find it easier to say no to them because they already know that we love them.

Creative grandparents make an unflagging commitment to finding new ways to say "I love you." We accept this biblical principle as our mandate: "My little children, let us not love in word or in tongue, but in deed and in truth" (1 John 3:18).

One way we can show our love is by mail. When on vacation, take the time to send a postcard to each of your grandchildren. Make sure to mail them separately. Preschool children seldom receive personal mail, and they are thrilled when Mom or Dad reads a card sent personally to them.

After a trip to the Grand Canyon, my wife Judy and I were greeted with these words from our granddaughter: "You wrote a letter just to me. I saved it and put it up on my wall." Her father reported that the arrival of that letter was the highlight of her week—and it took us only five minutes to write and mail it. Our now-twenty-four-year-old granddaughter still has all of the postcards we sent her when she was little. They sit in a box in her studio apartment in Chicago.

Another way creative grandparents show their love is by reading to their grandchildren. In a world of, "Hurry up! Get your coat on! I told you to go potty five minutes ago. Weren't you listening? Come on, we're late," grandparents need to slow down to be with their grandchildren. We have the time to read them their favorite story—again, and again, and again.

Children have a profound need to be spoken to and heard. We build trust and self-acceptance in our grandchildren simply by listening as they chatter on about anything and everything that pops into their active little brains. We may have been raised under the basic tenet of "children should be seen and not heard," but we believe that this robs kids of a chance to learn and build confidence.

Our youngest granddaughter, Kendall, loved to talk and jabber. She would often enter into adult conversation to give her opinion on matters. One day when Kendall was in the middle of one of her discourses, she abruptly stopped and said, "What am I saying? I don't know what I am talking about so I will just be quiet." She was right; she did not know what she was talking about. We let her go on and on anyway (she was so cute using big people's words). When she made her statement she laughed at herself, and we could not help but laugh with her. The memory makes us all laugh to this day.

## Tip #2: Look and Listen

Pay close attention to your wonder-years grandchildren. Observe them carefully. Listen to what they say. Learn their habits and idiosyncrasies. Then show them that you value them by acting on your understanding of the little things that make them tick.

Grandpa Jim is on the board of his church. People need to see him. But he aggravates some of the people at church. Why? Because when they are looking all over for him after the service, he is not available. They invariably find him in his grandson's Sunday school classroom (with Mom's and Dad's permission). He will be sprawled on the floor, eye-to-eye with little Christopher, listening to an account of a trip to the supermarket with his mom. This is his grandson's time, and he doesn't let anyone rob him of it. He feels that he is applying these words of Christ: "Let the little children come to Me and do not forbid them; for of such is the kingdom of heaven" (Matthew 19:14). Jim feels that since Jesus esteemed the little ones, so should he.

Creative grandparents build time into their schedules to listen to their grandchildren. One grandmother likes to take hers out for lunch, often to a place of the child's choosing. Okay, the child usually chooses McDonald's. But the child who is given the opportunity to choose is being sent an important message about her worth, her value as person. Besides, these lunch dates open up wonderful opportunities for conversation, and the most amazing things surface.

"Going for a ride in Grandpa's red truck" has become a great adventure for another set of grandchildren. It may be only a Saturday morning trip to the hardware store, but a stop at the donut shop gives Grandpa time to listen. He has found that his wonder-years grandson and granddaughter both enjoy these jaunts.

Grandma Susan is an artist and spends most Sunday afternoons painting with her granddaughter Heather. Five-year-old Heather often gives her paintings an "abstract" quality by bleeding the paint all over the page. Susan always lets her granddaughter know that her paintings are beautiful, and any mistakes she makes are the "happy mistakes" that come with creativity. Heather glows when Susan praises her paintings and takes the time to work with her.

When you listen to your granddaughter talk about her friend Jenny or her latest adventure at preschool, you communicate volumes to her. You tell her that she is important and that her experiences and feelings are significant. As you treat her opinions and interests with value, you are telling her that she has great value.

The wonder years are vital in a child's acceptance of his or her sexual identity. Grandparents can help with this very important aspect of development. When a grandmother applauds her "little man's" athletic exploits, or admires how much he looks like Daddy or Grandpa in his jeans and flannel shirt, she helps him see and accept himself as male. And Grandpa helps his granddaughter frame and appreciate her feminine identity when he says, "My granddaughter Kelsey's the prettiest girl in the whole church." Or, "My, you are just beautiful in that dress." Conversely, this time is crucial to reinforcing the aspects of their personality that are not stereotypically gender-specific. When Madeleine shows an interest in sports and climbing trees, or when Tyler loves to help Grandma bake, the interest should be encouraged. Encouragement of these activities shows an acceptance of your grandkids, whether they perfectly fit the mold of what a little boy or little girl is typically interested in or not.

Looking. Listening. Conversing. Sure, it's an effort to find the time and to get down to their eye-level. But doing so pays rich, rich dividends for them—and for you.

## Tip #3: Encourage and Answer Questions

Wonder-years grandchildren are always pondering the complexities of life. They have difficult questions that need satisfying answers. Mom and Dad can't answer them all. Grandparents can help.

Just as God listens intently when we ask, seek, and knock through prayer (Matthew 7:7), so we need to focus our attention on the asking, seeking, and knocking of our grandchildren. And just as God gives, helps us find, and opens in answer to our prayers, so we need to answer our grandchildren's many questions.

Children deserve truthful answers. Their natural, insatiable curiosity is the engine that powers their learning. True, we may get tired of the incessant questions of a two- or three-year-old. We may become frustrated trying to explain the innumerable complexities of our world to an inquisitive four-year-old. But they have a need to know and a right to know. Besides, if we keep answering, they'll keep asking, right on through the important—and difficult—teenage years.

Five-year-old Kendall was unusually quiet, deep in thought. After a few minutes she asked a serious question that was weighing heavily on her mind. "Grandpa, I don't understand divorce. What is divorce about?" That question deserved a response of equal seriousness, and I gave her an age-appropriate answer. Asking questions is one of the important ways children learn, and when we brush off their questions or treat their questions flippantly, we send children the message that they are not important.

How frustrating it can be for us when they are in the "why" stage! It goes something like this:

"Grandpa, why are there trees?"

"Because God loves beautiful things. He made the trees to make the world beautiful. And because they make oxygen."

"Grandpa, why does God love beautiful things, and what is oxygen?"

"Because beautiful things make His children happy, and He wants us happy. Oxygen is what we breathe."

"Grandpa, why does God want us happy? And why can't I see oxygen?"

"Because He loves us."

"But, Grandpa, why . . ."

This kind of conversation appears to be pointless, especially if it's repeated every time you get together. But it's of great value to that child. She wants to learn about her world, and she has chosen you to show her the way. Grandparents may grow weary of all the questions, but we will gain a second wind if we remember what a privilege it is to be selected by our young explorer as his or her navigator through this troubled world.

The next time you spend a few hours with your wonder-years grandchild, try asking questions that require more than a yes or no answer. You may get a lot of "what" and "why" questions in return, and you may exhaust yourself explaining everything from waves and wind to jet airplanes, but you'll have opened wonderful doors of discovery for your grandchild. And you'll have the opportunity to share your wisdom, experience, values, and faith with your exploring, questioning, learning little loved one.

## Tip #4: Take Risks

Paul, a successful businessman, was afraid of crying children. He found himself growing tense whenever he was around children who cried. He could control his business world with comparative ease, but he could not control a little weeper. He just did not know how to quiet them. As a result, Paul was afraid to be left alone with his infant grandchildren. Besides, his granddaughters were very attached to their mothers, which is a good thing. But for Grandpa Babysitter, it was *not* a good thing.

So how did he find himself with this tiny screaming bundle—with no woman around to help? Simple. He asked for it. This brave executive decided, fearfully, to be an involved, creative grandparent, and crying babies came with the territory.

He tried reading to her: still crying. He sang to her: cried louder. Played patty-cake: looked at him like he was crazy and resumed screaming. Nothing worked. After two hours it was officially crisis time. Finally he set all fear aside and picked her up. He held her gently to his shoulder and talked to her quietly. The roar became a sob, and then a sniffle. Then came the gentle, rhythmic breathing of sleep. He had done it! Few things in his life could have given him so much pride and satisfaction.

Paul chose to overcome his fears, and he felt as much sense of accomplishment in getting his granddaughter to sleep as he would have had in closing a $60 million deal. Yet he would have never experienced that joy if he had played it safe and refused the opportunity to conquer his fear of crying babies.

The doorway to loving every moment with our grandchildren is sometimes blocked by our apprehensions. Many of our fears are irrational or based on pride. Creative grandparents learn to step over those fears and build an intimate relationship with their wonder-years grandchildren.

## Tip #5: Say Yes More Often than No

It's all too easy to form the habit of saying no when you are asked to be an involved grandparent.

"Dad, will you watch the children this weekend so Jodi and I can get away?"

"No, Ken, I'm too busy."

"Grandpa, could you swing me?"

"We were just outside. Find something else to do."

"Grandma, will you color with me?"

"Not right now, honey. Grandma's watching television."

Saying yes more often than no means seizing every reasonable opportunity to be with your grandchildren. They only move through the wonder years once. This special time in their lives is flying past, and creative grandparents must make use of every opportunity to be with them.

Certainly there are times when it is appropriate to say no. But this should never be simply because it would inconvenience you to say yes. Grandchildren are not an inconvenience; they're a treasure. Time with them is not wasted; it is invested.

When the opportunity rises to say yes, take it. Look for ways to give positive responses to your grandchildren. They need it, and you need to see their eyes light up.

## Tip #6: Be Your Child's Playmate

When you play with your grandchildren, you will open the windows to their souls. A game of hide-and-seek reveals their fears and sense of fun. A game of chase shows their excitement. A session of drawing and painting will unleash their creativity. Playing dollies will show you their needs and values. A game of whiffle ball or plastic-pin bowling will show you their motor skills. And all of it reveals their language, thought, and moral development.

Play can also open wounds on your body. As I write, I can still feel my hurting ribs, a painful reminder of summer play with my grandchildren. The formula was simple: a family get together + a new Slip 'N Slide + Grandpa = DISASTER.

A Slip 'N Slide is a strip of plastic with a sprinkler system built in to wet down the surface. The object is to run, launch yourself into the air, and skid on your chest the length of the plastic. Whoever slides the longest distance wins. Unbelievable fun!

They were outside; I was in. Soon, chants of "Grandpa! Grandpa!" echoed through the house. I reluctantly donned my bathing suit. Then I charged out of the house, achieved full speed, and dove onto the wet plastic. I slid, covering the full length, and continued to slide onto the lawn, sailing through the mud and grass. I stopped six inches from the sidewalk. Grass and mud were in my eyes, bathing suit, mouth, and hair. The discomfort was not eased as I heard the children's shrieks of laughter. I still hold the family record for the longest slide!

Being your grandchildren's playmate doesn't necessarily require a ride on the Slip 'N Slide. It does mean setting aside the newspaper, putting aside the book (even this one), and doing what they want to do. Balancing the checkbook can wait when the children are begging to play.

Playing with your grandchildren shows them that you love them and appreciate who they are. Creative grandparents treasure these moments because it gives them a peek into their grandchild's world. More importantly, playmates are friends—and that's what you want to be to your grandchild.

Jim is a retired construction worker. He has become good at Old Maid. Why? Because that's the only game his granddaughter wants to play. So he gets lots of practice. Jim is a moose of a man, tall and weathered by the elements. The cards, which look like miniatures in his hands, look enormous in his granddaughter's. As they play, his eyes belie his years. They dance with delight whenever she picks the Old Maid and tries not to show it.

Jim has many opportunities to be his granddaughter's playmate. They could do all kinds of things. Old Maid is their special kind of play. The only limit is the imagination and energy of grandparents, and their desire to see their wonder-years grandchildren light up the house with laughter.

Play is always a learning process, but not in a rigid academic sense. Wonder-years children learn how the world works through play:

- Play fuels their imagination and creativity.
- Play helps them learn the rules of social interaction.
- Play gives them a legitimate outlet for their natural exuberance.
- Play gives introverted children a safe opportunity to reach out to others around them.
- Play gives wonder-years children a way to express themselves.

Say YES to play!

## Tip #7: Follow the Child's Agenda

Have you ever seen a grandmother being pulled around by her four-year-old grandson and wondered who was in charge? Don't wonder too much. That grandma is probably a creative grandparent who knows that doing what she wants is important, but doing what he wants is imperative.

Be willing to do what your grandchildren want to do and talk about what they want to talk about. Sure, it's frustrating to read a five-year-old the same story over and over again. But after that fifteenth reading, when she begins to read it back to you, you understand the reason for her request.

Because you realize that your agenda may have nothing to do with theirs, ask them what they want to do. Even if it doesn't excite you, you need to do it every once in a while. Let them pick the restaurant. Let them choose the game. Let them order their choice from the menu.

Our family participates in an activity we call *"bummin' around."* We define it as *creatively doing nothing somewhere else.* It's an activity widely practiced by grandparents who think creatively. The beauty of it is that the grandchild gets to set the agenda.

One day the agenda was garage sales. Lauren took $1.50 from her piggy bank, and we embarked on a quest to find a suitable treasure. (I was along merely to drive the car.) Several hours later, after traversing nearly every square mile of our city, we found an appropriate item: a shell necklace of dubious origin and even more questionable aesthetic value. Lauren purchased it for the bargain price of seventy-five cents and proudly presented it to Grandma as a gift that evening. Grandma was delighted to be remembered. Lauren and I still talk about our garage sale experiences during her wonder years.

Creative grandparenting means following our grandchild's agenda. At stake is their sense of importance and self-worth.

## Tip #8: Love Jesus with Your Grandchildren

"Dear Jesus, thank you for this terrific day. Thank you for giving us life. Thank you for loving us. And Jesus, thank you for Erin. Please watch over her and protect her. I love her very much too. Amen."

"Grandma, why did you ask Jesus to take care of me?"

"Because I love you very much, and I don't want anything bad to happen to you."

"But why did you ask Jesus? Does He care about me too?"

"Yes, Erin. Jesus loves you very much. The Bible says that Jesus loves you so much that He died for you. That's a lot of love!"

"Does Jesus know my name?"

"I know He does, Erin. He knows my name too and He loves you as much as I do."

Children develop their first perceptions of God during the wonder years. They try to picture Him in their minds. They become aware that their parents and grandparents read the Bible, pray, go to church, and try to follow Jesus. Creative grandparents know the importance of modeling a real and personal relationship with Christ.

Living in obedience to God and His Word, with Christ a part of everyday conversation, makes a powerful statement about the reality of your faith to your grandchildren. They know what Grandma and Grandpa believe because they watch you so closely. You cannot fake it for very long in front of them. Do you see what this does? It gives you the responsibility of forging a real-live faith of you own, lived out with all its complexities and ambiguities, for their questioning, impressionable minds to see.

The Bible testifies to the power of this kind of faith in a grandparent. When the apostle Paul charged Timothy with the task of carrying out the work of the gospel, he wrote, "When I call to remembrance the genuine faith that is in you, which dwelt first in your grandmother Lois and your mother

Eunice, and I am persuaded is in you also . . ." (2 Timothy 1:5). Love Jesus with your grandchildren. There is no greater way to care for them!

Creative grandparenting for the wonder years is:

1. Loving your grandchildren all-ways.
2. Looking and listening.
3. Encouraging and answering questions.
4. Taking risks.
5. Saying yes more often than no.
6. Being a playmate.
7. Following their agenda.
8. Loving Jesus with them.

Creative grandparents are always making up their own guidelines, continually finding new ways to show love to their wonder-years grandchildren. As you live creatively with your grandchildren, you will have stories of your own, stories of delightful, meaningful, wonder-filled moments because you chose to be a creative, involved grandparent.

The following list gives creative grandparents ideas for activities to do *with*, not *for* their wonder-years grandchildren. Some activities are relatively inexpensive and easy; others are more costly and for some grandparents more difficult. Begin with an activity that you feel comfortable doing, and then take a risk and try some activities that stretch you and make you step out of your comfort zone. Don't feel that you need to do all of these activities. Enjoy your grandchildren all-ways!

## 25 Creative Things to Do with Your Wonder Years Grandchildren

1. Tell them stories, real or imagined.
2. Go shopping with them and buy them one inexpensive toy after allowing them to play with several in the department store toy aisle.
3. Watch movies together that are age-appropriate.
4. Explore your backyard or park, looking carefully at flowers, shrubs and bugs. Take a large magnifying glass along.
5. Create works of art such as clay sculptures, paintings, or crafts.
6. Explore the wonders of nature by visiting special exhibits and interactive children's museums.
7. Play toy instruments together like kazoos or horns.
8. Have a tea party with them and their dolls or stuffed animals.
9. Sing or say nursery rhymes and songs.
10. Play on the floor with them. Wrestle, and let them win.
11. Find a nature trail next to a stream or lake. Look for frogs and other aquatic life.
12. Do a puppet show together.
13. Go out for an ice cream cone.
14. Play memory games like the online Celebrity Simon or Match It.
15. For older preschoolers, build them a tree house in which to play games, or build a snow fort with them in the winter.

16. Have them help you bake cookies. Let them mix the cookie dough.
17. Take them to a farm or a petting zoo to observe and pet the animals.
18. Play house or store with them. Don't buy a playhouse or store. Create them with a sheet stretched over some chairs, or an appliance box.
19. Go to the beach and spend the day making sand castles.
20. Play hide-and-seek with them.
21. Go to the library and let them pick out a few books and read them.
22. Practice writing out their name with them.
23. Help them make a card for their parents.
24. Do a treasure hunt.
25. Walk along a path or beach collecting rocks or shells.

# CHAPTER 3

# Coaches and Cheerleaders

Jeffrey walked hesitantly into the living room, his head down and his hands in his pockets. Grandpa looked up from his paper and saw that his eight-year-old grandson was looking sad. "What's wrong Jeff? Are you okay?"

"Grandpa, nobody cares about me."

"What do you mean? Of course they do. Your mom and dad love you."

"I know they love me, but it just seems like everybody else is more important than me and comes first. John is starting high school, and Mom and Dad are always talking about his good grades and how good he is in sports. Jenny is three, and everybody always says how cute she is. All they do is yell at me to get out of the way or go clean my room."

Grandpa pondered this for a moment, and then said, "Jeff, come here a minute. I want you to know something. Your grandma and I love you very much. We think that you are the best, and we are so glad that you are our grandson. How would you like to spend a week with me on the sailboat this summer? Just you and me, sailing Lake Michigan together. I've already talked to your mom and dad about it, and they said it would be okay if you want to do it. I'll teach you how to navigate and be at the helm, steering the boat. We might even cross Lake Michigan to Wisconsin."

"Yeah! You can teach me how to sail and we can fish off the back, and we can make hot dogs for dinner!"

"Yes, we can do all of that. Let's go talk to your mom about it."

Children ages six to eleven can sometimes feel left out. Teenagers get all the press and toddlers get all the attention. Children in the middle can feel left out or in the way. Creative grandparents know that school-age children need as much attention during these years as any other time in their lives.

In this chapter we will look at what drives our children—what makes them tick in their crucial school-age years. What are the developmental tasks for children ages six to eleven? What do children of this age need most from a creative grandparent? We will also identify the pitfalls of these years and see how we as creative grandparents can help our grandchildren avoid them. And we will examine closely the roles we can play to best support them.

## Child Development

Get ready! Be prepared! Your grandchildren often will make a mess of things during these years. They will take things apart and not be able to put them back together. They will get things out and not put them away. The curiosity of children grows sharper during middle childhood. Their "whys" become never-ending and their curiosity boundless.

I remember those years in my life, growing up on a farm. My father had just purchased a new hand-propelled cylinder lawn mower with the meager savings he had set aside. I looked at that mower in amazement and decided, for some reason unknown to this day, to take it apart. I managed to completely disassemble the mower, and then I couldn't remember how to put it back together. My father had to take the mower to the shop and order new parts to replace the ones that somehow disappeared. Looking back, I believe that experience may have been my first lesson as a mechanic. In recent years I have rebuilt my Porsche 911 engine and several other engines, although occasionally there are parts left over, which has become a running joke for my family.

We will understand the reasons for our grandchildren's curiosity once we identify the developmental tasks of early childhood. We define a developmental task as the major task each child needs to accomplish during a certain age span to grow up healthy and to function well in society. Achieving this task enables him or her to move successfully into the next developmental stage. In one sense, the developmental task becomes the job of the child during a particular period in his or her life. The job or task of the school-age child is to develop a sense of self-sufficiency and competence.

During these years our grandchildren begin to build a sense of accomplishment. They find out whether or not they are able to compete successfully with other children. Once they reach these elementary school years, children are not protected as much by their parents. They are finding out whether they will be able to make it in the big, wide world.

Using the phrase "industry versus inferiority," psychologist Eric Erickson discovered that children of this age need to find out what they can do—what they are good at. This helps build a sense of competence. If, in the process of trying to build competence, they are continually ridiculed and put down, they will develop strong feelings of inferiority. These rambunctious, energetic kids are extremely fragile.

Ten-year-old Sarah was crying as she ran into the house. Her breath came in short gulps and tears cascaded down her face. Her nose was running. She looked pitiful. "Sarah, what's wrong?" her mom asked. "Why are you crying? Are you hurt?"

"Mom, the kids are so mean to me at school. The boys call me names and I don't have any friends."

"What do you mean, you don't have any friends? Just tell me what happened."

"I was trying to play basketball in gym class but I'm so bad at basketball. No matter how hard I try, I can't catch the ball or shoot it or pass it to the right person so *they* can shoot it. They picked teams and I was the last one picked! I knew nobody would want me on their team! Then while I was playing, I prayed and prayed that nobody would pass the ball to me. But they did, and I dropped it and accidently kicked it out-of-bounds. We lost the game. The winning players laughed at me and my team was so mad at me. Mom, I feel so bad—I don't want to go to gym anymore. Why can't I be good at something? Everything I do turns out wrong."

Sarah is struggling with issues of competence. In her world, playing basketball is an important skill and she just can't measure up. That failure is producing a strong sense of inferiority in her. Sarah is beginning to believe that not only is she not a good basketball player, but that she really is not good at anything. Universalizing is common with school-age children. Because they fail in one area, they immediately apply that failure to their entire lives. Of course some of us adults are also guilty of this.

An important aspect of building a sense of competence and self-sufficiency is learning to get along with peers and competing appropriately with them. During their preschool years, most children have been shielded from intense competition. Mom and Dad have helped their children learn to share with other children, face competition, and handle failure. However, when the child is in school all day, the parent is not there. She has to do it on her own, and this can be traumatic.

Perhaps, for example, other kids can swing all by themselves, but Jeremy has always had Mom push him. When the bell rings for recess and the children head for the swings, Jeremy is in trouble. He can't compete. Other children are performing at a higher level than he is. This erodes his self-esteem. However, if Jeremy is doing well in his schoolwork, his inability to swing with the other children is offset. Jeremy is compensating for a weakness or lack of ability in one area by doing something else well.

During these school-age years, children begin to compare themselves with their peers. In early childhood Mom and Dad did all the comparing, wondering if Johnny was tall enough, smart enough, or developing fast enough. Parents (and grandparents) were competing with other parents (and grandparents). However, in these school-age years, children see for themselves how they stack up against other children. They need to be able to point to something in their lives that they can do as well as their peers, whether it's athletics, music, or scholastic achievement.

My son Jack was never a great athlete. In elementary school the popular game was kickball, and he was terrible at it. Oh, he kicked the ball all right, but he couldn't catch it. He was afraid it would hit him in the face, so he closed his eyes before he tried to catch the ball. His friends always picked him last for kickball teams. They laughed at him and it hurt.

Jack compensated for his inability to measure up in kickball by becoming very good at dodgeball. His natural quickness and fear of the ball served him well in a game where the object is to avoid getting hit. Though Jack blushed at his failures in kickball, he could take pride in his success in dodgeball. This illustrates the importance school-age children attach to successful competition. Grandparents would be wise not to underestimate the importance of building a sense of competence in their grandchildren.

We have been talking mainly about physical skills, but this principle applies equally to cognitive and social skills. During this time children are always trying to determine who is the smartest student, the best athlete, the prettiest girl, or the most popular boy. Therefore, it's helpful for children who are not good athletes to do well in their schoolwork or in some other area in which they can demonstrate competence. It's okay to have lots of friends but not be great at spelling.

Some children, however, feel that they are not good at anything. They have *no* sense of accomplishment in their lives. When they look at themselves, they see failure. Instead of achieving competency, they fall into feelings of inferiority. And that's where creative grandparents can really help.

As we formulate a plan to help, we need to be aware of the three areas in which our grandchildren need and welcome our help. First, we can help our grandchildren build a sense of competence by becoming their *coaches*. Second, we can help them build a healthy sense of self-esteem by becoming their *cheerleaders*. Third, children need encouragement as they formulate their ideas of right and wrong, good and bad. To help our grandchildren learn to accept limits and rules, we sometimes need to become *umpires*. Let's look at each of these roles more carefully.

## Grandparents as Coaches

How do grandparents help their grandchildren become competent and develop a sense of self-sufficiency? As creative grandparents, we spark our grandchildren's innate abilities by joining their team and becoming their coaches. Most of us can point to significant adults who took us under their wings and passed along a skill to us when we were young. They gave us confidence by building our competence. We need to show our grandchildren how to do something and help them to do it well.

Grandpa Joe is taking seven-year-old Christopher camping this year for the first time. Joe is a skilled hiker, hunter, and camper. He spends his leisure time outdoors, in tents and on the trail. This summer Christopher will begin learning how to be a competent camper. Joe plans to teach him how to set up a tent, pack a backpack, cook over an open fire, and other skills necessary to survive in the wilderness. Chris is a shy child with few close friends. Imagine the boost to his self-esteem that will accompany his newfound competence as a Grandpa's camping buddy! Grandpa Joe is a creative grandparent who understands his grandson's need for a coach.

As coaches, we help our grandchildren build competence and become self-sufficient in two ways. The first and most obvious is by our instruction. Coaches pass along skills to their young apprentices.

When my sons Jack and Jon were in elementary school, they spent a portion of almost every summer with their grandfather. He was a celery farmer, and every year he taught his grandsons a new skill. Jack will never forget the summer he was first allowed to pack celery on the assembly line. He thought it was the greatest thing in the world. Standing there with his gloves on amid the teenagers and adults employed by his grandfather, he felt competent and grown up. He felt as though he was doing something worthwhile and useful. My father was acting as a coach, instructing my sons in the ways of farming. Although neither boy had a desire to spend his life as a farmer, both gained a great deal of confidence from their summers with their grandpa.

Coaches are instructors, but they are not cruel taskmasters. Grandchildren do not need to be pushed into anything. They don't need to be used so Grandpa and Grandma can relive past glories. They should not be ridiculed when they fail, or punished if they lose interest. The image of the good coach should conjure up the idea of gentle and patient love. As coaches, we are more interested in the process than the outcome, more concerned about the game than the score. Our goal is not to produce world-champion farmers or campers or swimmers or whatever. Our goal is to produce grandchildren with a quiet, growing confidence in themselves that is bred by competence and nourished through small successes.

The second way we coach our grandchildren is by allowing them to fail. Our success-oriented culture leaves little room for failure. Yet we know that failing almost always precedes growth and improvement. Our grandchildren may not have anyone else in their lives who let them fail and then encourage them to get back up and try again. A good coach doesn't expect his player to get it right the first time or the second, or maybe even the tenth. Coaches allow for slow growth, characterized by three steps forward, two steps back. After a granddaughter fails, she may be down on herself, frustrated by her inability to learn the skill, or discouraged by her inability to complete the task. As gentle coaches, we can pick her up, dust her off, and send her back into it again. If she knows that failure is part of learning, part of life, the pressure to immediately succeed is replaced by a desire to persevere.

Creative grandparents look for opportunities to coach their grandchildren. Every grandparent has skills and abilities to pass on. Your grandchildren need a sense of competence and confidence that your coaching can provide. Don't wait around for the perfect opportunity. Create that opportunity. Pick up the phone to call or text your grandchild. Invite them over, and get to work.

## Grandparents as Cheerleaders

As our grandchildren grow up, plenty of people will be ready and willing to tell them what is wrong with them. Your grandchild will already have a good sense of what he or she is not good at. Years of being put down by friends and family are not easily forgotten. Chances are, however, there aren't enough people who tell your granddaughter how great she is, or who tell your grandson how wonderful he is. As creative grandparents, it is our blessed privilege to be cheerleaders for our grandchildren.

Not only is a sense of competence important for school-age children, they also need assurance that the things they do are accepted by significant people in their lives. As creative grandparents, we certainly are among those significant people, and we can be the ones with the loudest voices cheering them on.

Some time ago we read about this kind of grandmother. She was cheering on her eleven-year-old grandson. It was field day at school, and everybody was running and jumping and racing. Her grandson was running the hundred-yard-dash, and she was on the sidelines, her gray hair blowing in the breeze. She was shouting his name over and over again. "Go, Mark, you can do it. Go! Go! Go! I know you can make it, Mark." She was urging her grandson on at the top of her lungs.

Her grandson had one good leg; the other was a prosthesis. He was running dead last. The other runners had already finished. But she loved her grandson, and knew he would benefit from completing the race. After he crossed the finish line, he went over to his grandma and hugged her. He didn't let go for almost two minutes. "I did it, I did it. Thanks for being here, Grandma. I love you, Grandma."

Every one of us needs our own private cheerleader, but especially during these important school-age years. So, look for something your grandchildren are doing well and praise them for it. Pay attention to them as they begin to develop abilities, and then give them sincere affirmation. Let people know that you think your grandchildren are the greatest in the world, and let them know it too.

Children who pass through these school-age years without building an adequate self-image enter adolescence at a severe disadvantage. Some of them won't make it through their teen years. They'll give up. Or they'll drop out of society. They may make bad decisions in high school regarding sexuality, drugs, and alcohol. It is imperative that children enter the stormy years of adolescence with someone in their corner rooting for them, cheering them on, building their self-esteem.

It isn't hard to be a cheerleader. All it takes is a little time and a lot of enthusiasm. Remember, our grandchildren have a good idea about what is wrong with them. But they may not have anyone dedicated to telling them what is right about them. Accept the assignment! Be a cheerleader for your grandchildren. Not only will you help them accomplish the developmental tasks of their school-age years, you will boost them into adolescence and adulthood with healthy self-esteem.

## Grandparents as Umpires

The third aspect of the task of our school-age grandchildren is the refinement of self. One of the most important facets of the search for self-sufficiency is the formulation of values and development of a system of morality. Children are not only trying to figure out where they fit on this planet, but also how they should act. Deciding what is right and wrong, and learning how to determine good from bad, plays a large part in their thinking. Because school-age children often can't articulate their feelings well, we can easily miss this important aspect of their development. Teenagers can be much more articulate in expressing their feelings, so we are more aware of their faith and moral convictions. With preteen children this is often a hidden process, but it is still very important.

People who counsel troubled teens know that many of them did not develop a system of morality during childhood. Parents looking back on those years say, "He was such as quiet child, so accepting of everything we said. Now look at him! He has turned his back of God and gone his own way." More likely, the truth is the child never did own his parents' values. He was just going along because it was easy. His value system was never challenged or completed. Therefore, we must not take for granted that this important task of exploration was achieved.

A corollary to moral development in our grandchildren is their understanding of limits and rules. Children in this stage of life are learning to live with self-imposed rules and limits. We call this personal morality. They are also learning to live within societal boundaries and family rules and limits. This is not always a painless or uncomplicated process. The natural ego and self-centeredness of children isn't easily tempered by rules. Coming to terms with limitations on behavior can be a long, difficult process, but it is a vital part of development. Learning to act and react within societal and family boundaries is necessary to function successfully as an adolescent, and later on as an adult.

As children succeed or fail in their attempt to build competence and a system of morality, they modify their self-image accordingly. This will have a profound effect on them during adolescence. Children who enter the teenage years with a shaky self-image are not likely to exit with confidence or security. Unless preteens complete these developmental tasks, they will face a difficult transition into young adulthood.

So what does all this mean? What difference does this developmental task stuff make to creative grandparents?

First, it is important to us as we try to understand our grandchildren. We need to know what they are going through and what should happen next in their development. We need to empathize with them and support them as they struggle to complete each developmental task.

Second, when we understand what is happening during these years, we are better able to develop a plan to help our grandchildren make it through times with a healthy sense of self-esteem and a solid system of morality and priorities. Our grandchildren are learning to act and react within societal and parental limits. To help our grandchildren accomplish this task, we need to become umpires.

When some people go to baseball games, they watch sluggers and try to guess who is going to hit one out of the park. Other people are looking for a great fielding play. They love to watch double plays turned with style and efficiency. Still others like to watch the coaches and the manager flash signs to their players. Not me. I like to watch the umpires. I think they have the toughest job in baseball. They have to enforce the rules of the game. They have to make split-second decisions about what is a ball and what is a strike, who is safe and who is out. They do this with thousands of screaming fans hurling abuse at them, and knowing that players and managers will second-guess them. Yet the best umpires never lose control. They calmly make the call and let the chips fall where they may. Highly paid and higher strung athletes may argue and complain, but to no avail. The umpire has made his decision.

In many ways our role as umpire in the lives of our grandchildren is similar to baseball umps. We help our grandchildren play within the rules and understand the limits. Just as baseball umps have to deal with pleading athletes, we have to deal with children who don't always see the wisdom behind the guidelines.

Our job is to help our grandchildren establish a system of morality and live within it. The question, of course, is how? How do we help our grandchildren develop and work out their values? How can we encourage them to play by the rules and stick within societal and parental limits? The answer is threefold. First, we must model a moral lifestyle. Second, we must grab the "teachable moment" that helps them see the reasons behind the rules. Third, we must call them out when they step beyond the boundaries.

We cannot overestimate the value of modeling behaviors and attitudes before our grandchildren. Nowhere is this more important than in the area of personal morality. As our grandsons and granddaughters make their way through the school-age years, they are slowly putting together a system of values. They do this in large part by watching how the significant adults in their lives act in key situations. That means our grandchildren are watching us to figure out what is right and wrong, and that can be pretty scary. The old saying that "your talk talks and your walk talks, but your walk talks louder than your talk" is true—especially with your grandchildren during these important years.

Fairness is a major issue with children this age. Listen to them, and you will hear their conversation punctuated again and again with cries of, "That's not fair!" When we fail to walk our talk, our grandchildren may not say it aloud but inside they are crying out, "That's not fair. You make me live by one set of rules and you follow another. It's just not fair!" Our grandchildren will see the inconsistencies. Just as a batter becomes angry at an umpire who moves the strike zone around, so our grandchildren will become angry when we say one thing and do another. We cannot hold them to standards of morality that we don't adhere to ourselves. It doesn't work to say, "Do as I say, not as I do." Grandchildren will end up doing what we do, regardless of what we say.

Our biggest concern with our school-age grandchildren is that they take steps to follow Jesus during this formative time. More than anything else, I want my grandchildren to learn obedience to Christ. To help them do that, I must make sure they see me live that way. I can talk about God all I want, but if my grandchildren don't see me back it up with my life, it will be to no avail. They'll know it isn't real. We pray every day that we will live consistently for Christ in front of our grandchildren. We ask God to help us as we try to live like Jesus before them.

Our second role as an umpire is to help our grandchildren see the purposes behind the rules and the reasons behind our values. We do this by taking advantage of every teachable moment we can. When they are with us, we have opportunities to use incidents and experiences to illustrate why there are rules and limits on behavior. A pastor took his grandson with him on an out-of-town speaking engagement. On the way home, they stopped at an unfamiliar restaurant and ordered dinner. Before it arrived, a man seated near them began to get obnoxious. His voice grew louder, and soon he was yelling obscenities. The man was drunk. The boy was about ten years old, and he had never seen an intoxicated man this close before. He listened and watched, and then asked, "Why is that guy doing that, Grandpa?"

"Because he's drunk, he doesn't have control of himself." The boy looked at his grandfather and said, "Now I know why you don't ever want me to drink." They talked for the next ten minutes about God's view of self-control and what the Bible says about drunkenness. That was a teachable moment, and the boy was able to see the reasons behind the rules.

If our grandchildren don't see those reasons but instead see rules as arbitrary and unfair, they will fight them. They may continue to struggle as they move on into high school and adulthood.

Teachable moments come often. Not all of them are as obvious as the one above, but each one gives us a chance to explain the need for values and the reasons behind the rules. We can take those moments and use them to help our grandchildren complete their developmental tasks.

Our final responsibility as umpires is to call our grandchildren into account when they need it. I'm not talking about discipline here, but rather the gentle nudging of a developing conscience. When they err, we must not look at our grandchildren as if they have just committed the unpardonable sin. Instead, we should gently guide them back into right behavior and thinking. Unlike baseball umpires who scream at the top of their lungs, "YER OOUUTTT!" grandparents whisper into the ears of their grandchildren, "Hey, look where you're standing. I think you're out-of-bounds."

Lauren was sometimes difficult to deal with as a child. She was always pushing at the boundaries and questioning them. She needed to be reminded often that she was out-of-bounds, that she had two strikes and was in danger of swinging and missing again. Sometimes her grandpa wanted to holler, "YER OUT!" because her actions had upset him or were bothering him. But when he looked at how fragile she was, and remembered that she was just learning about making the right decisions, he toned it down. He slid up alongside her and whispered so no one could hear, "You're stepping out-of-bounds." It was usually enough for her to see that she had moved outside the lines. By treating her with respect and letting her keep her dignity when he called her out, he enabled her to maintain her self-esteem while building her values and morality.

The school-age years are vital to the growth and development of our grandchildren. Helping them complete their developmental tasks during these years is a high calling and a tall order. But we can do it. We can help our grandchildren build a sense of competence and self-sufficiency. Creative grandparents are just the right people to help children find confidence and develop life skills. As a counselor, I have seen grandparents work miracles in building their grandchildren's self-esteem. I've watched seven-year-old blue eyes light up when their grandparents become their number-one fans. I've seen children blossom under the gentle, yet firm imposition of limits and rules. I've watched patient, loving grandparents carefully explain the purpose behind those rules to their grandchildren. I have enjoyed watching grandparents model the Christian ethic consistently with integrity.

Yes, we can help our grandchildren achieve the developmental tasks of this stage of their lives. We can help them overcome their feelings of inferiority and develop competence. But it takes a creative plan. It takes our willingness to understand our grandchildren and then to become their coaches, cheerleaders, and umpires.

In order to model behavior, grab teachable moments, and gently correct, we need to spend time with our grandchildren. The following list gives creative grandparents ideas for activities to do *with*, not *for*, their school-age grandchildren. Some activities are relatively inexpensive and easy; others are more costly and for some grandparents more difficult. Begin with an activity that you feel comfortable doing, and then take a risk and try some activities that stretch you and make you step out of your comfort zone. Don't feel that you need to do all of these activities. Enjoy your grandchildren all-ways!

## 25 Creative Things to Do with Your School-age Grandchildren

1. Learn to downhill ski or water ski.
2. Teach them how to shoot a BB gun or .22 rifle, or teach them archery. Be sure to include gun-safety instruction.
3. Buy a chemistry set and experiment.
4. Take a river canoeing trip. Teach them how to maneuver using the paddles.
5. Hike in the woods or mountains or go on a bike ride.
6. Teach them how to hunt or fish, and then go on a hunting or fishing trip.
7. Learn horsemanship and ride together.
8. Visit garage or estate sales in your neighborhood. Teach them monetary values and how to discern quality of merchandise.
9. Teach them how to cook and make a special meal for the family.
10. Introduce them to wilderness camping by taking an overnight backpacking trip in the woods or mountains, or tent camp for a few days or a weekend.

11. Bird-watch. Identify various birds by sight and sound.
12. Take a boating safety course.
13. Play interactive video games (e.g., Wii).
14. Purchase a couple of inexpensive kites and fly them on a windy day.
15. Make up humorous stories about the origin of names of cities through which you travel.
16. Have an ongoing chess competition.
17. Go to county fairs, carnivals, and circuses.
18. Plant and tend a flower or vegetable garden.
19. Share a hobby such as photography, ceramics, or knitting.
20. Attend a sporting event.
21. Have them sleep over and do a movie night. Watch their favorite movies.
22. Have them teach you a game and play it.
23. Build a model ship or airplane.
24. Learn a sport together.
25. Teach them their multiplication tables.

# CHAPTER 4

# Fear Not, the Best Is Yet to Come

Lynn was in tears. Only sixteen years old, and her life was falling apart. None of her friends at school understood her, and they turned on her on a dime in an argument; her parents were constantly nagging her; and her first boyfriend broke up with her and started dating her best friend. All of the things that are important to a teenage girl—acceptance, popularity, attention from the opposite sex—were not working out for Lynn. And to make it worse, her parents gave her a hard time about it: "Why don't you bring your friends over more often? You're living like a hermit. All you do is spend time on your computer. What's wrong with you? Your grades are pretty disappointing this semester. We know you can do better. If they don't improve over the next marking period, we're going to take away your car."

Lynn *knew* that her grades were poor. But couldn't her parents see that she was doing the best she could? And how could she explain her feelings to her mother, who was beautiful and never had braces and had been a cheerleader in high school? Even though she was living through what everyone told her were the best years of her life, she felt desperate and alone.

Lynn was crying when she opened the familiar oak door that led into her grandmother's home. "Lynn, what's the matter? Come on in. I am so glad to see you. I was wondering this morning how you were doing; I haven't seen you in a few weeks. Let me pour you a cup of coffee, and you can tell me why that beautiful face of yours looks so sad."

Perhaps it was the familiar smell of her grandmother's house—fresh coffee, disinfectant, and garlic (a combination that doesn't sound pleasant but was). Maybe it was because Grandma never talked down to her but always treated her as an equal, as an adult. Maybe it was the understanding she heard in her grandmother's voice, or the laugh lines around her grandmother's mouth, or her timeworn hands.

Whatever it was, Lynn felt immediately at ease. Her feelings tumbled out in a jumbled rush of sobbing words. Then her tears were gently wiped away by those loving hands. And even though her problems were not gone when she left Grandma's kitchen, they had, somehow, become manageable again. Her grandmother's six-and-a-half decades had put her teenage difficulties into perspective. Lynn's grandma told her about the girls who had teased her in school, whose names she could no longer remember. And about the first boy she dated, who no longer had his two front teeth. Looking into that deeply lined face, Lynn knew that she would be able to withstand even the most difficult of high school times. Lynn's grandmother did not realize how important she was to her granddaughter that morning, but her role in Lynn's teenage years was unique and extremely valuable.

Adolescence is a time often feared by parents and grandparents. They have heard horror stories about rebellious teenagers, the drug culture, and teenage pregnancy. For some adolescents, this is a difficult time, a "stormy" period of life. But for the majority of teenagers this is not so. Studies show that most teenagers love their parents and want them to be an important part of their lives. Most parents actually enjoy watching their children make the transition from dependency to independence. Grandparents especially can eagerly anticipate this period in the lives of their grandchildren.

Even if grandchildren are going through a difficult time, often they will turn to grandparents for advice, encouragement, and comfort. This is a great opportunity for creative grandparents to be involved in their lives.

A 2009 Oxford University survey about grandparent/grandchild relationships has shown just how much grandparents contribute to a grandchild's well-being. Not only do teenagers value intergenerational bonds, but grandparents' active involvement produces better adjusted adolescents. This study by Ann Buchanan and Julia Griggs involved over 1,500 children, ages eleven to sixteen, in schools around England and Wales. Grandparents taking part in grandchildren's hobbies and interests was linked with fewer emotional, social, and behavioral problems. The study linked high levels of grandparent involvement in single-parent families with fewer adjustment difficulties for the children in those families. When families experienced difficulties, young people sought emotional and other support from their closest grandparent, and this support improved their well-being. Grandparental involvement also was associated with more considerate and sensitive young people who were more willing to help others. Further, grandchildren wanted contact with grandparents, even if parents prohibited it, or if law did not support grandparents' rights to such.

Teenagers often turn to grandparents for advice, encouragement, and comfort when experiencing difficulties or discouragement. Being a teenager is both wonderful and terrifying. It is wonderful to grow into a strong young man or lovely young woman. It's great to get that first job and driver's license. But it can be terrifying to learn how to deal with budding sexuality, to grow faster or not as fast as peers, or to be shaking inside when everyone else seems calm and completely together.

It's tough to be a teenager in the twenty-first century. Today's adolescents are being pulled in hundreds of directions. Commercials are saying, "Buy this soft drink or wear this brand of clothes and you'll be acceptable." Parents are pushing for good grades and college and career decisions. Peers are partying, drinking, and having sex. Adolescents have to sort out for themselves who to listen to and what type of people they want to become. It is an isolating, lonely time.

To better understand this time in your grandchild's life, take time to read about adolescence. Learn what teenagers are like and what they are going through. Understanding adolescents makes it a whole lot easier to be sympathetic with them, even when they are not acting responsibly. Learn as much as you can about this special group of people, and love them unconditionally.

## The Task of Adolescence

The primary task of adolescence is to form a sense of identity. During the teen years, young people strive to differentiate between themselves and their parents. They define and identify their own beliefs and goals. Between the ages of twelve and eighteen, they develop a strong sense of self.

In addition, teenagers are doing something for the first time that we grandparents have been doing for years—thinking abstractly, thinking in terms of concepts and ideas. They are gaining the ability to compare and decide, to make value-laden choices and deal with the consequences. And learning how to do that can be traumatic.

When Ethan was eleven he was bright, enthusiastic, funny, and enjoyable to be around. He liked church and seeing his friends there. He would often hug his dad and give his mom a kiss, telling them that he loved them. But by age fourteen, Ethan was not the same kid. He went from bright to overbearing, from enthusiastic to loud, from fun-loving to sarcastic—in short, from enjoyable to surly.

The difference was that Ethan was beginning to think for himself. He was sorting out his values from his parents. He was also comparing them with his mental image of ideal parents. Needless to say, they fell well short, as we all do. It was a difficult time for Mom and Dad. They worried about the kind of person Ethan was becoming.

Grandparenting teenagers like Ethan can be frustrating and intimidating. But it can also be exciting and rewarding. So many grandparents simply stop trying to be involved with their adolescent grandchildren, choosing to wait until they "grow out of it." Teenagers need more people on their side, not less.

Young children see their grandparents as gift-givers and playmates. When those children reach their teen years, that role concept changes. Teens struggle with basic life questions. They ask themselves, "Who am I? Where do I fit in to the world around me?" Facing these questions may cause them to distance themselves from their grandparents. Quite frankly, most teenagers don't appreciate anyone telling them how to live. Our gifts and antics, which they once saw as special or amusing, now strike them as corny and childish. No more trips to the zoo or playground. Grandparenting teenagers, therefore, requires greater effort, more discretion, and more tact than grandparenting younger children.

Don't let that scare you away from being the creative, involved grandparent of a teenager. True, grandparenting teens can be more work than it is for children, but it's worth it. Teenagers have a profound need to be loved and accepted unconditionally. Creative grandparents are especially good at doing that. Teenagers also need a sense of continuity, of connection with the past, and grandparents are walking history lessons. Teenagers need to develop interests and skills that establish uniqueness and identity, and grandparents have a lifetime of experience and a variety of abilities from which to draw.

Creative grandparents of teenagers must assume four important roles if they are to help their grandchildren get through the confusing, crucial, formative years of adolescence: teacher, family historian, facilitator, and friend.

As teachers, creative grandparents can pass on the wisdom and skills acquired and honed over a lifetime. They can take the time to teach their grandchildren how to bake an apple pie or build a birdhouse. They can tell them how to apply for a job, use and take care of tools, or patch up a strained relationship.

As family historians, creative grandparents connect their grandchildren with the past and give them a feeling of continuity. Teenagers struggle to build a sense of identity. Unless they understand where they came from and how they fit in, they will have difficulty deciding where they want to go.

As facilitators, creative grandparents communicate to their grandchildren what Mom and Dad were like when they were teenagers. This clears the way for deeper understanding between parents and teens. When they hear about the foibles and ill-starred adventurers of their parents, teenagers find it easier to identify with and understand them. When they learn of their parents' accomplishments, they feel pride and are challenged themselves. They see Mom and Dad more completely and more realistically.

As friends, creative grandparents provide what teenagers consistently say is their deepest need, acceptance and love. Teenagers need grandparents most when they do the things that are least acceptable, and when they are the most unlovable. I think it is best summed up with a statement Erin made during a conversation about acceptance: "Grandpa, I know you will always love me, no matter what I do." It doesn't mean we will always approve of her behavior, but we will unconditionally love her. Also, as a friend, the play times become activity times. We add the coffee shop to the ice cream shop. Our conversations include opinions and even instruction from the grandchild to the grandparent. This role of friend will continue as they grow into adulthood.

## Grandparents as Teachers

The woods were cold and silent. From the blind deep in the forest, Ed could hear the wind make its way through the stand of pines off to his left. The sharp crack of a twig snapped his attention forward, where a black squirrel was scurrying from tree to tree. A muffled yawn broke the stillness. Ed saw that Kyle, his fourteen-year-old grandson, was struggling to stay fully awake. "What's wrong, Kyle? Was getting up at 5:30 too early for you?"

"Grandpa, I don't know how you get up this early every day. I can hardly keep my eyes open."

"Do you want to go back to camp and take a nap?"

"No. I'm tired, but I'm not going back. I've wanted to do this since I was a little kid. No way am I bailing out now."

Ed chuckled to himself. He thought back to when Kyle was a little boy begging to go deer hunting with Grandpa. "You can go when you're fourteen, Kyle. I promise."

"But I'm never going to be fourteen, Grandpa. It feels like a million years away."

Ed often wondered how the years could fly by so fast. It was wonderful to have the boy with him on this brisk November morning for his first deer hunt. He had shown Kyle how to build a blind. He had given him lessons in identifying deer tracks and reading deer signs like rubs and scrapes. He had taught him how to shoot calmly and, hopefully, accurately.

Ed's reverie was broken by a crunch and a flash of brown and white from the corner of his eye. It was unmistakably a white-tailed deer. "Kyle, look over there," he whispered urgently. Kyle rustled as he turned around in the blind. "Grandpa, it's a deer! I think it's a buck."

"Sure is, Kyle. Look at that rack! Okay now, line him up in your sights. No quick movements."

"But Grandpa, you saw him first." Kyle whispered hoarsely.

"I've shot plenty of deer, Kyle. Today it's your turn. Put your scope on him and follow him in your sights. Do you see him?"

"Yeah, I see his antlers. They're huge!"

"All right. Take a deep breath and let it out slow. Aim just behind the shoulder. Pull easy. Don't jerk the trigger."

CRACK! The report of the rifle reverberated through the woods. "Grandpa, he went down. I got him!"

"Good shot, Kyle. Now let's go find him and field-dress him. It looks like your Mom is going to have to learn how to cook venison."

"That was awesome, Grandpa!"

Ed watched happily as his ecstatic grandson ran to the animal, and then he proudly took his picture.

A week or so later, relaxing in his recliner, Ed reflected on his many deer hunts—at least one a year for fifty years. This was by far his most satisfying ever—and he never fired a shot.

It was a very special moment between a teenage boy and his grandfather. As teacher, Ed filled a need in Kyle's life. He passed on interests and skills that had been handed down in the family for generations. It gave him the opportunity to share a special, memorable moment with his adolescent grandson. And Ed's grandson revered him for his knowledge of the outdoors and his wealth of stories and experiences.

Filling the role of teacher can be a source of great satisfaction to a grandparent. Rarely will you feel more needed than when your granddaughter, just blossoming into woman-hood, looks up at you from the garden and asks, "What do we plant next, Grandma?" Teenagers need to become proficient at something. They need to be able to point with pride and say, "I did that," or "You'll never believe what I did yester-day!" Gaining a skill fills a need to be good at something, to be different from everyone else without having to step out into bizarre, rebellious acts of nonconformity.

You may be asking yourself, "What do I have to offer my teenage grandchildren?" How about a lifetime of acquired skills? What are you good at? Do you sew? Teach your grand-child. Do you fish? Take your fifteen-year-old princess out for a couple of hours on the lake and make her bait her own hook. Do you cook or bake? Invite your grandchildren in for a cookie-making party. Do you work with wood? Can you draw? Paint? Do you collect anything? What skills have you learned through your vocation? Were you a nurse or admin-istrative assistant? A tool-and-die man or a construction worker? It doesn't matter. You most likely have a skill your grandchild would like to learn.

Creative grandparents need to keep a few things in mind as they teach. Don't insist that your teenage grandson learn to play the viola just because you loved it when you were a kid. Remember tip #7 from chapter 2: Follow the child's agenda. That principle holds true for adolescents as well as toddlers. Let them choose. If they are interested in something you know nothing about, guide them to someone who does know, or take a crash course yourself. My granddaughter Elena wanted to learn how to ride a horse; I (Jerry) had no idea how and no experience riding horses, so we took lessons together. Later, when I needed a companion to travel with me to Arizona to go into the Grand Canyon, guess who went with me on horseback into the canyon for five days?

The only way to discover what your grandchildren would like to learn is to listen to them. Not just once, not just for a few minutes, but repeatedly and often. Some teenagers are afraid to reveal their personal thoughts. Even such an innocent desire as, "I'd really like to learn to sail like Grandpa," can remain a painfully guarded secret. These longings are closely tied to their identity, and adolescents are not about to let just anyone into their souls.

Teaching your teenage grandchildren will take perseverance, creativity, energy, and love. The return on the investment, however, is incredible. As creative, teaching grandparents, you can be one of the few welcomed into the inner life of a teenager, all because you shared a special knowledge or skill that helped your grandchild build identity.

## Grandparents as Family Historians

Whenever an elderly person dies, a library burns down. This old saying is true. As people grow older, they accumulate knowledge of the past. When they are gone, that knowledge goes with them. Creative grandparents can be veritable libraries of history, especially family history. Our role is to remember what has gone before—to know everyone in our family who did something important or embarrassing, and why.

This fits perfectly into the teenager's task of identity formation. It helps with the questions, "Who am I?" and "Who do I want to be?" One reason today's teens are struggling so mightily with the task of forming an identity is that they have lost a sense of connection with their families. They sense no continuity with the past. Researchers have different theories about the reasons for this, but they agree on one important point. If teenagers are to form a healthy sense of identity, they need to know where they came from and how they fit into family history. Creative historian grandparents connect them with the past and provide them with the continuity they are longing for.

As the librarians of family history, grandparents are much like the typical school library: neglected. Our teenage grandchildren have to be enticed to use us. Just as the teenager with the important research paper does not necessarily spend her evenings in the library, so the teenager in search of identity needs motivation to use her grandparents. As creative grandparents, we will have to motivate our grandchildren to learn family history from us.

How, you may ask, do we accomplish that? The cliché answer is, "Very carefully." But I'm not being flippant. Dealing with teens requires patience and perseverance. You might start by giving snippets from the past when the situation calls for it. You can't force history and knowledge on anyone. And, history is often boring to students. I remember every history class in school as being taught by a very boring teacher. We must make our family history come alive and present it to our grandchildren with excitement and exuberance.

Christmas might be a good time to begin. "I remember Christmas Day, 1951. I had cold C-rations for dinner. Pretty near froze to death. I almost got shot that day."

What grandson could resist asking, "Grandpa, where were you? You almost got shot?"

"I was in Korea, John. We were fighting the communists of North Korea. I thought I was at least a hill or two away from the enemy. So I walked around, kind of carelessly. But the North Koreans reminded me that communists don't believe in Christmas by using me for target practice. As I dove for cover, I thought, *You idiot! Don't you know any better?*"

Sharing tidbits of historical information will catch the imagination of your grandchildren and may leave them asking for more. "He drove up on that motorcycle, sideburns blowing in the breeze, and looked so sexy in his black leather jacket. He also had a convertible, which really turned me on. All I could think was WOW, I am going out with him even if it kills me."

"Grandma, I can't believe you said that!"

"Grandpa was a hunk."

"Grandma, you really felt like that about Grandpa?"

"Of course I did. I was young once too."

As grandparents relate the pieces of the story every family has, their teenagers will begin to feel a sense of their place in the world. They will start to understand what went on before they came along, and how they fit into the family picture. It makes their task of building identity much easier. Without them even being aware of it, you will have helped your grandchildren accomplish the most important task of adolescence.

As family historians, you would be wise to follow these guidelines:

*Tell the truth!* That may seem obvious, but truth can be slippery and difficult to maintain. We are tempted to leave out stuff that is, well, embarrassing or indecorous. Yet Ephesians 4:25 warns us to "put off falsehood and speak truthfully" (NIV). Grandparents who edit the family history to protect certain sensibilities are hurting their grandchildren. A fourteen-year-old girl is reassured to know that her grandmother had a huge crush on a cute guy in the ninth grade, but she never found a way to tell him she liked him. It helps for Grandpa to tell that he got a D in algebra, or that he lost his driver's license because he did not obey the speed laws. It brings grandparents and grandchildren closer, and it helps teens identify with their grandparents.

*Resist the temptation to create heroes.* The temptation always exists to make things better or worse than they actually were for the sake of the story. Your grandchildren should be able to count on you to tell the truth. If you do go off into a tall tale (and I think that's always your right as a grandparent), find a way to let them know where truth ended and fiction began.

*Allow for a remote control attention span.* Grandparents must realize that many teenagers today have restless minds that flit from one thought to the next. It is increasingly difficult, especially for young adolescents, to concentrate for long periods of time. They are people weaned on cartoons and used to watching ESPN and reality TV, where the picture changes every three to five seconds and they are never more than five minutes from a commercial. And while watching their programs, they are texting their friends. Talking three hours straight just will not work for them. Tell the family history in short episodes. Keep them interested, wanting to hear more.

*Ask for a response.* Help your teenager get involved in the story. You might ask if they have ever wanted to do something like that, or if they have ever felt that way. Once they start talking, let them go on. You are getting valuable inside information. Remember, telling the family history is a means to an end. The goal is identity formation, and a growing trust between grandparent and teenager is a valuable by-product.

*Weave your faith in Christ into the story.* If you are a Christian family, a history that excludes God is incomplete. Teenagers need to know that faith works. They need to know that it is possible to live as a child of God in spite of very real human failings. Fill your history with the story of God's love. Tell them how His hand was on your life. Don't force it. Don't preach your faith to them. Just say it with the conviction in your heart. One grandmother received Christ at a small country church when she was still a girl. Years later, she vividly described to her granddaughter the music, the preacher, and the one who prayed with her to receive Jesus. She told how her faith helped carry her through the long, tough days of the Great Depression. Her granddaughter listened carefully; she was struggling with an important decision, though her grandmother did not know that. The grandmother's story of faith led her granddaughter to obey Christ on a critical issue.

## Grandparents as Facilitators

"I think the best thing about Grandma is the way she tells stories about Dad. She tells me what he was like and what he did when he was my age." These words from a fifteen-year-old girl describe the role of facilitator that creative grandparents can assume.

Adolescence can be a time of strain between parents and children. Even the strongest, most loving families go through difficulties when their children become teenagers. When our son Jack was sixteen, he challenged us constantly. He was always testing us, to see how far he could extend the boundaries. Jack was not a bad kid—not at all. He was normal. We were not bad parents. We were normal. But our normal reactions sometimes created friction, and friction can erupt into anger and arguments.

During these years, Jack often went to visit my father (usually to pay back money he had borrowed). Now, Jack could have mailed him the money. But talking to Grandpa and Grandma Schreur was special: it meant getting the low-down on Dad, and there was a lot to get!

My mother and dad would relate the struggles they had with me when I was a teenager. I was a rebellious teen, always in trouble. I was in and out of jail. I drove recklessly and fast. Hearing about this from his grandparents made a deep impact on Jack. My mother wept as she told about her wayward son, wondering if I would kill myself or someone else in my car, or get shot by the police. As she talked, Jack was deciding that he was not going to put his mother through the same thing.

Jack later told me that listening to my parents' stories helped him better understand me and my parenting style. My parents had become facilitators, helping my son understand me.

Some parents are not willing to let their teenagers see them as real people. Perhaps they are afraid of losing control or respect. As creative grandparents, we can tactfully bridge that gap, not by interfering, but by honestly telling it like it was.

Two dangers must be avoided by grandparents as facilitators: 1.) We must not use this role to get back at our children for unresolved conflicts. It would be easy to use the role to criticize our children (their parents) or put them down in front of their children. Grandparents need to resolve those conflicts appropriately with their children. 2.) We are not to use the role to manipulate our grandchildren or undermine their parents. Grandparents must never use their grandchildren as weapons in a power play. Teenagers are too fragile and too precious to be misused in that manner. Please be careful. It's all too easy to fall into this trap. We tell our grandchildren about our children—their parents—not to get even with them but to help them and their teenagers understand one another.

Just as important, we must not misuse the facilitator role by manipulating our grandchildren into an "us versus them" mode—us against their parents. We are striving to bring understanding, not discord. We must speak about their parents with the highest respect, and we must support their decisions. We also need to let our children know what we are telling our grandchildren about them and why. This will prevent misunderstanding and suspicion.

One grandparent told his grandson about the great disappointment in his father's life. He had wanted to go to college to study architecture, but the war and finances prevented it. That seemed to give the boy direction, and it helped him understand his father. The young man later graduated from Purdue as an architectural engineer. He fulfilled his father's dream, and found great satisfaction in his career.

As facilitators, creative grandparents strive for better understanding between parents and teens. While we are building that understanding, we are also drawing our grandchildren into a vital relationship that adds enjoyment to our lives and strengthens their personal identity and connection with the past.

## Grandparents as Friends

Most grandparents want at least to be familiar with their teenage grandchildren. Yet the role many desire most is that of friend. Fulfilling that desire can be slow, difficult, or even impossible. We want from our adolescent grandchildren open, trusting relationships, but they do not always want the same from us.

Consider Sarah, a vital, energetic, sixty-five-year-old grandmother. Her five grandchildren are just about the dearest things in the world to her. Sarah is troubled about her oldest grandson, Adam. Adam is fourteen, and he doesn't want to be around her anymore. Although she seldom lets it show, she is crushed by his refusal to come near her or let her kiss him on the cheek, always ducking out of her embrace.

Sarah felt terrible on the family's annual vacation trip to Florida over spring break. In previous years they had played games together in the motor home. They were silly traveling games mostly, like "slug bug" and "most states on license plates." But on this trip Adam sat sullenly in the corner and stared blankly out the window—all the way to Florida. Once they got there, he wasn't much better. Adam was always trying to get away from the family and go off on his own. He even refused to go for ice cream with Sarah, a long-standing vacation tradition.

When the trip was over, Sarah told her story and asked, "What did I do wrong? What can I do to get Adam back?" The answer: Nothing. Adam is simply being an early adolescent.

While forming that all-important sense of identity, teenagers need distance and freedom. Sometimes we are sure that they are cutting themselves off from the family, but that is usually not the case. They are lengthening the cords. And the reason is no mystery. Even though teenagers need to feel connected, they also need to find out who they are apart from their families. This confusing process can leave Mom and Dad frustrated and bewildered. The same is true of grandparents who love that teenage grandchild and want to be his friend. These grandparents must recognize that they are not being rejected. They can still have a deep and meaningful relationship with their teenage grandson. But the timing must be on his terms.

Three principles for becoming friends with your teenage grandchildren are wait, accept, and shelter. Let's look at each of them.

*Wait.* To wait for our grandchildren is to give them the time and space they need to figure out who they are and who they will become. If we demand closeness now, we will drive them away, perhaps forever. We must be patient and persevering, waiting for them to come back to us. Grandchildren usually create this sense of distance between the ages of twelve to fifteen. Then, from ages sixteen to eighteen, they may gradually close the gap again. Younger adolescents are still working through their task of identity formation, while the older ones have become secure enough in themselves to inch back into a close relationship with Grandma and Grandpa. Older adolescents often want friendship with their grandparents. We must realize that by waiting, we are letting them grow up. When they come back, they do so as "almost adults." Because of their newfound reasoning skills and maturity, along with a growing self-confidence, they are more delightful to be with than when they left. They distance themselves as anguished children and return as young adults. Be patient. Let them do what they have to do. And above all, don't give up on them too soon.

*Accept.* Do teenagers ever feel completely accepted? Television commercials push them to desire the perfect face, the perfect body, the perfect hair, the perfect figure. As our teenagers compare themselves with the images on the flickering screen, they are left with the impression that they are not good enough. They do not measure up to the ideal. They are not a "ten." Because adolescents are struggling through deep issues of image and self-esteem, they are vulnerable to exploitation. Some teens will do just about anything for that feeling of safety and security that accompanies acceptance. This "fitting in" process can be as simple and harmless as a weird hairstyle or an absurdly expensive pair of sneakers. Sometimes it's deadly, involving alcohol, lawlessness, sexual activity, and drug abuse.

Creative grandparents can accomplish wonders with their teenage grandchildren by accepting them for who they are and loving them regardless of their behavior. This, of course, does not involve condoning destructive or immoral behavior. What we must communicate to them is that our love and acceptance is unconditional. It is not based on outward appearance or achievements, but on relationship: "You are my granddaughter. I will love you forever, regardless of your success or failure, your appearance, or your actions. To me you are always beautiful, and you are always mine. And I'm glad and proud to claim you as my granddaughter."

Matt was an excellent athlete and a good student. He was popular with the other teenagers and accepted by everyone. But then he got thrown off the basketball team for drinking. Suddenly his friends on the team didn't have time for him. Soon Matt felt alone, rejected by everyone. Later he described the important role his grandparents played during this critical period:

My grandfather and grandmother never stopped caring about me. After school, while my friends were at basketball practice, I would feel very down and alone. So I walked over to Grandpa and Grandma's house. Grandma never yelled at me about the drinking. She knew that I knew it was a stupid thing to do. Instead, she listened to me as I talked about anything and everything. She and Grandpa were the only ones who did not treat me differently after I got thrown off the team. They, especially Grandma, loved me all the way through it.

This is creative grandparenting at its best. It provides a listening ear and unqualified acceptance to adolescents trying to figure out this oftentimes cold, uncaring world.

Our granddaughter Erin went through a phase in which she left nothing unpierced. It seemed for a while that every time we saw her, she had a new piercing—ears, nose, belly button, you name it. Her parents were visibly annoyed and distressed, but we tried to put it into context—of all the forms of experimentation, this was fairly harmless and reversible. And, truth be told, she actually looked pretty cute with a nose ring. She knew that we didn't think any less of her because of this new style, and she remained open and honest with us because she could trust us.

*Shelter.* The Old Testament emphasizes a concept that personifies creative grandparenting. In Israel there were six cities of refuge (see Joshua 20). If an Israelite accidentally killed someone, he could flee to these cities for safety. Tribal law and custom demanded that someone who killed another be killed in return: "A life for a life" (see Exodus 21). But this was not fair in the case of an accident. To protect the innocent, God established cities of refuge throughout Israel. Someone who accidentally took the life of another could go there for refuge. The people of the city were obligated to protect him.

As creative grandparents, we want to befriend and help our grandchildren through the teenage years. One thing we can do is turn our home into a "city of refuge" for them. We can provide a place for them out of harm's way. We can protect them and offer them safe-keeping. The Bible describes it this way: "When he flees to one of these cities, he is to stand in the entrance of the city gate and state his case before the elders of that city. Then they are to admit him into their city and give him a place to live with them. If the avenger of blood pursues him, they must not surrender the one accused" (Joshua 20:4–5 NIV).

Creative grandparents are sanctuaries; our homes are cities of refuge to our adolescent grandchildren. We offer them a place to which they can flee when they feel that their world is crashing down around them. I have an image of myself standing at the city gate and telling my granddaughter's pursuers, "Stop! I have her now. You cannot harm her anymore." Then, I see those seeking to harm my granddaughter turn away empty-handed. She is safe in my arms and secure in my home.

Creating a safe atmosphere will endear your teenage grandchildren to you forever. They need a place of refuge, a sanctuary. You can provide it. And in so doing you can teach them about God, who is their stronghold through all of life (Psalm 27:1).

Lynn's grandmother loved her precious granddaughter. She accepted Lynn and provided a place of refuge for her. Now, years later, Lynn still gets a lump in her throat when she talks about her grandmother. "Grandma changed my life," she says. "So many times when I was alone, she was my friend. I could not have made it without her. And I bet she never knew it." Deep down inside, she probably did!

As creative grandparents, we can be friends with our teenage grandchildren. But we must be willing to wait for them to come to us. We must not push them into a relationship they do not desire. We must always be available to them. We must accept them for who they are, and remember that teens often struggle with low self-esteem and feelings of inferiority. We can communicate an unconditional love that does not fade with time or distance. Grandparents who wish to be friends with their teenage grandchildren can become cities of refuge in a cold and hostile world. Our homes can be sanctuaries in the storms, lighthouses in the darkness, places of safety and love for our struggling adolescent grandchildren.

The following list gives creative grandparents ideas for activities to do *with*, not *for*, their adolescent grandchildren. Some activities are relatively inexpensive and easy; others are more costly and for some grandparents more difficult. Begin with an activity that you feel comfortable doing, and then take a risk and try some activities that stretch you and make you step out of your comfort zone. Don't feel that you need to do all of these activities. Enjoy your grandchildren all-ways!

## 25 Creative Things to Do with Your Adolescent Grandchildren

1. Teach them to drive a car (with their parents' permission).
2. Ask them to help you set up or install software programs on your computer.
3. Let your granddaughter style your hair.
4. Take a road trip, just the two of you. Borrow or rent a sports car to make it more exciting.

5. Shop with them for clothes.
6. Grow a vegetable garden. Donate or sell the veggies. Or if you are hungry, eat them.
7. Take a train trip across the U.S. or to a major city.
8. Rock climb, rappel a cliff, or wall climb.
9. Go on a mission trip to a third-world country.
10. Serve in a soup kitchen or homeless shelter.
11. Design their dream trip, and take it.
12. Hunt big game animals (e.g., deer, bear, antelope, elk, moose).
13. Spoil your granddaughter at the spa.
14. Ride the five highest roller coasters in America.
15. Read through the Bible in one year.
16. Research and write your family history.
17. Attend baseball games at every American or National League stadium in the country. Begin with those nearest you.
18. Restore a classic car together and let them drive it when completed.
19. Attend a concert of their choice.
20. Attend their favorite university's basketball or football game.
21. Have them accompany you on a business trip.
22. Visit their favorite amusement park.
23. Spend a week or weekend at a summer cottage or resort.
24. Visit culturally distinct neighborhoods or communities.
25. Go river rafting down your favorite river.

## CHAPTER 5

# On Their Own

Two years ago on a chilly October morning I (Erin) called my grandparents. I call them often, so this was not unusual, but I had never made this kind of phone call to them before. After graduating from college, I had traveled Europe for three months, and now I was broke. I needed money, and I needed it immediately. I had been offered a job in Chicago, but I had no way of paying the security deposit or the first month's rent for an apartment. I had less than a week to come up the money so I could start a new life in a new city.

I could have asked my parents for the money, but since I moved back home our relationship had grown tense. After four years away at college and months traveling overseas on my own and with friends, I was having a hard time reintegrating into family life with two younger siblings, a family pet that needed care, and chores around the house. I was eager to get out on my own, but I did not want their help to do it. I have always been stubborn and proud, two things that can be disastrous in combination. So I turned to my grandparents.

My grandparents are generous, and they taught me that generosity was something to express in all areas of life, whether it be giving money, love, kindness, friendship, or time. Their history of generosity did not change the fact that asking them for a substantial sum of money was going to be difficult. Everything in me wanted to pay the bills myself to prove that I could handle the adult world I was on the verge of entering.

When my grandma picked up the phone, she greeted me with her typical warmth, "It's our Erin girl. How are you, honey?" I relaxed slightly while we made small talk. She congratulated me again on landing the job, and then said, "You know to ask us if you need help with anything, right?" I cringed, realizing that it was time to ask her about borrowing money.

"Well, Grandma, I do need your help. I need money to get an apartment and I don't have time to save up for it and since my trip I've been broke and I really don't want to ask my mom or dad because we haven't exactly been getting along. Would you and Grandpa consider loaning me some money for the move to Chicago?" She chuckled at the rush of words that revealed my nervousness and said, "I'll talk to Grandpa and call you right back." They ended up loaning me the money, and I have been in Chicago, in my tiny one-room apartment, ever since.

As young adults, our relationships with the world are becoming deeper and more complex, and our relationships with our grandparents follow suit. Practical, adult concerns like money and leases and careers have suddenly emerged. Yet we are, in no small measure, still wide-eyed children following our grandparents around outdoors and asking endless questions. However, now we have entered a deep part of the forest, often dark, with a meandering path that we occasionally lose. As we walk this sometimes scary path, we wonder if this is the right way, if this is the right time, if this is the right job, if these are the right friends, or if this is the right place to live. The caring voice of our grandparents guiding us out of the forest is more important now than ever before.

## Emerging Adulthood

I am in what psychologist Jeffrey Arnett has called the "emerging adulthood" phase of life, between ages nineteen and thirty. I am no longer a teenager, but I am not a traditional, full-fledged adult. I don't own a home, I'm not married, and I don't have children. Arnett writes in *Emerging Adulthood*, "Having left the dependency of childhood and adolescence, and having not yet entered the enduring responsibilities that are normative in adulthood, emerging adults often explore a variety of possible life directions in love, work, and world-views." I know there is a great deal to see and learn and experience in this world, and I am hungry for all of it.

This time is confusing and terrifying and exciting. Arnett writes, "Emerging adulthood is a time of life when many different directions remain possible, when little about the future has been decided for certain, when the scope of independent exploration of life's possibilities is greater for most people than it will be at any other period." The stakes are much higher for emerging adults than when we were teenagers. We have real jobs on the line, we are in debt with student loans, and we have an entire world in which to get lost. We also lack clear models for how this part of our lives should look. Our grandparents, and many of our parents, had children and careers by their twenties. Expectations for us are not entirely clear.

Jorie typifies this phase. Jorie is twenty-five, a poet, and recently finished a master of fine arts degree at a prestigious university on the East Coast. She did not expect wealth to come with this newly acquired degree. But she also didn't think she would have to move back in with her parents, and neither did they. Jorie loved and got along with her parents, but there was tension between them. They wanted her to quit her restaurant job and get an "adult" job. She wanted to write but knew she would not have the time and energy to work on her writing after a nine-hour day in the office. Her parents thought she was being spoiled and unrealistic.

Jorie and her grandfather had always been close. From the time she was a little girl, they had gone on long walks together. When it was too cold to walk, they went out for a bowl of soup at the nearest diner. She told him about her dilemma: Should she give up a lifelong dream that she had prepared for with years of school, or disappoint her parents? Her grandfather had only this to say to her: "Jorie, who you are will not change, no matter which path you choose. And the fact that I'm proud of you won't change either. Do what you need to do; you'll always be my granddaughter."

Though not the concrete advice Jorie was hoping for, her grandfather's words reassured her that no matter what, whether she succeeded on her own terms or someone else's, her grandpa stood behind her. And the more she thought about it, the more she appreciated his response. It was, after all, *her* job to make decisions—but her grandfather's unqualified support for her as a person enabled her to really think through her choices.

Perhaps it is an outworking of our youth and inexperience, but each decision facing us feels oppressively important. Jorie's grandfather, with decades under his belt, understood what Jorie failed to recognize: that small, everyday decisions shape our lives, and the quality of our character is far more important than how we choose to earn a living. Jorie and I, and people like us, are fortunate to be able to explore and follow our passions. We are also fortunate to have those with more life experience walk with us and guide us.

The merits and consequences of emerging adulthood have been debated by many, including those in this age group. Much has been said about the failure of my generation to assume responsibility for ourselves and our future. Some say we are lazy, entitled, and uninterested in the toil that is required for success. While there is a measure of truth in those words, it is not the full truth. We are capable of leading meaningful, responsible lives.

Grandparents are in a unique position to reassure emerging adults that where we are in life is acceptable. They can tell us that they are proud of us, and we can believe them in a way we may not be able to believe our parents. Even if you, as grandparents, aren't excited about your grandchildren's dreams to travel the world, teach English in a developing country, or take unpaid internships, you are still able to love and support your grandchildren. Though these nontraditional plans may seem impractical, they are the ways in which we explore the world beyond the classroom.

Let's revisit Arnett's comment that "emerging adults often explore a variety of possible life directions in love, work, and worldviews." What can grandparents do to help grandchildren in these areas?

## Explorations in Love

Relationships are often more stable during emerging adulthood than they were in our teens, but most of us have not settled down with a committed partner. Many of my peers are delaying marriage or waiting to have children, postponing the lifestyle our grandparents were living already at their age. According to the 2010 Census, the median age for first marriages is twenty-six for women and twenty-eight for men. More young adults are waiting to marry until after completing college and graduate school. Some are children of divorce and struggle with commitment. Others want the nest egg before the nest. Still others are in an extended adolescence, not yet ready to make major life decisions.

As a single young person, I find that family members from older generations are often skeptical of the decision to wait to enter into those long-term, life-changing relationships. Disapproval of this decision does little to sway us toward responsible life decisions but does go a long way toward convincing us that something is wrong with us.

Unfortunately explorations in love don't always end well. Nearly everyone I know has a heartbreak or two behind them at this point; some of these relationships end better than others. When Cory and Rachel met the summer before she went to college, they were instantly inseparable. Each day, Rachel left her morning waitressing job and visited Cory at the hotel where he worked. She would bring him coffee or a bite to eat and sneak a kiss when his boss wasn't looking. At night they went to movies, went out for dinner, went swimming, had bonfires, talked for hours, and fell in love.

Cory was mild-mannered, sweet, and adored Rachel. Rachel was independent, feisty, and intrigued by him. They met each other's parents and friends, and Rachel introduced Cory to her grandparents, who liked him immediately. Rachel and Cory decided to stay together when Rachel left their Midwestern hometown for school in the fall.

Once at school in New York City, Rachel blossomed. She had looked forward to living in New York for as long as she could remember, and she loved every minute of it. She made friends from all over the world, went to plays, explored the city on her own every Saturday, and called Cory to tell him about each day. Cory, still in their small hometown and still working at the hotel, was a receptive audience for Rachel's stories at first. He was glad she was happy, and told her so every day, but with waning enthusiasm.

One Wednesday night in November, Cory called to tell her he would be in New York the next day. He wanted to surprise her for her birthday. When he arrived, she took him around the city and introduced him to all of her new friends.

On Sunday afternoon, when Cory was about to leave for the airport, they got into their first real fight. Cory hated New York, didn't like her friends, and could not understand how she could be so happy there, especially without him. Rachel took this to mean that Cory must really love her, since he couldn't stand to be without her, and was expressing normal insecurity and jealousy. Rachel acquiesced and told him she wasn't happy without him there, knowing that this would make him feel better. They made up and he left. Little did they know that this argument would set the tone for the next three years of their relationship.

After a cross-country move to attend schools near each other when Cory's jealousy became more than Rachel wanted to put up with, they moved in together to save on living expenses. The first month went smoothly, and they were giddy with their newfound sense of adulthood and stability. But the second month they began fighting every day. At first they bickered about small issues—whose turn it was to do dishes, or why they spent so much time with Cory's friends but never Rachel's—but eventually the arguments became more and more about Cory's excessive drinking and Rachel's need to control. During one particularly contentious argument, Cory threw Rachel to the ground. She continued to scream at him and he kicked her, pinned her down, and shoved her against the wall. Then he left.

In the hours that followed, Rachel stayed on the ground, unable to comprehend what had just happened. She eventually got up, packed a few things in a backpack, and went to stay at a friend's apartment.

When she awoke the next morning, her first instinct was to call her grandfather. He had been a social worker and substance abuse counselor before he retired, and was one of the most rational people she knew. He was a devout Christian and did not approve of her moving in with Cory before they were married, but he had never judged her. She knew she could trust him. If she called her parents, they would insist on flying out and rescuing her, but she was not sure she wanted to be rescued. She just wanted some perspective.

Her grandfather, whom she called Papa, picked up on the second ring. "Rach? Why are you calling so early on the weekend?"

"Papa, it's Cory."

"Is he okay? What's wrong? Did he hurt you?"

"He's okay, sort of. I'm not hurt, but we got into an argument last night, and it got pretty physical. What do I do, Papa? I love him."

Hearing his strong granddaughter sound so broken was almost more than his heart could take, but his years of experience, in life and in counseling, told him that she would get through this. He could remember what it felt like to be young and in love and understood the desperation Rachel was feeling. He walked her through the conversation she needed to have with Cory. He made her promise to call a local agency for help, and then two days later checked in with her to make sure she had made the call. He even offered her the money she would need to move out and get started on her own. Rachel didn't take him up on the offer of a loan—but she did accept his quiet advice and constant encouragement. And while she decided to stay with Cory for the twists and turns left in their relationship, when their relationship ended, and all of the tears had been shed and the lessons learned, Rachel pointed to her grandfather as one of the reasons she found the strength to leave.

The National Violence against Women Survey of 2000 found that one in every four women will experience domestic violence in her lifetime. This is not an insignificant number. Given the statistic, your granddaughter will need you and will need to know her worth in your sight. When she is at her lowest, she will need you to scoop her up, dust her off, and help her hold her chin up. Though the story of Cory and Rachel is an extreme example of a bad relationship, it is not uncommon for relationships to be turbulent and sometimes violent. These explorations in love are often very painful.

## Explorations in Work

Whether emerging adults are exploring career options, trying to make it through another day at dead-end jobs, or aspiring to start businesses, we need practical advice. Even if grandparents don't have experience directly related to our fields, years in the workplace have taught them valuable lessons that we want to learn.

One lesson grandparents can teach is the value of hard work. Our grandparents know how much effort is involved in doing a job well. One of the complaints I hear about my peers is that we possess no work ethic. While I do not think this is a fair accusation, emerging adults need to be reminded that entering the workplace and launching careers are not always easy tasks.

As a boy, Nate watched his grandfather tend his vegetable and flower gardens. For this kid from Brooklyn, toiling out in the sun caring for the land made no sense. The satisfaction, if it ever came, seemed minimal and was months ahead. Summer after summer, Nate watched his grandfather, until one summer when he was sixteen he finally asked, "Grandpa, what is there to like about gardening? It's tedious and dirty and often unsuccessful. Why don't you get a new hobby?" His grandfather replied, "I don't know. I guess I feel lost if I'm not working on something. And I love the smell of the dirt after a rain."

For his grandson, who had not yet worked a day in his life, this sounded absurd. Now, ten years later, he is beginning to appreciate his grandfather's words. The simple act of working, no matter the task or goal, can provide structure. And the satisfaction from a job well done can be more rewarding than tangible compensation.

Another lesson our grandparents can teach is job skills and knowledge. When I graduated from college, I pursued a longtime personal and academic interest in domestic violence and sexual assault survivor advocacy. I decided to volunteer at the local women's shelter and went through extensive training to be able to do so.

As a counselor with more than thirty years of experience, my grandfather had insight into what I was learning and what I would be dealing with as a volunteer. We were able to have long, peer-to-peer conversations about how best to help the women who visited the shelter. He knew things that I didn't, and I was able to share updated statistics and methods for dealing with situations. He had worked with women facing these problems and knew the kind of information that would be most helpful to them. Our shared work interests allowed us to experience a new way of relating. In addition to our grandparent-grandchild relationship, we developed a collegial mentor-mentee relationship.

Even if you and your grandchildren are not interested in related fields, you can still pass on your experience. Perhaps one of the most important lessons to teach your grandchild is the value of perspective when evaluating career choices. Previously work was passed down through a family. It was normal for a family to have several generations of blacksmiths, farmers, or carpenters. Those early days offered limited choice of a job or career. You just did what your father did. Today there are so many choices. It's like going to the supermarket to buy a bag of chips, only to discover twenty different kinds. Sometimes you walk away without making a choice—there are just too many options, and the decision becomes overwhelming. And that's just choosing a snack food! Think of life's large decisions, the ones with consequences that may affect you for the rest of your life. Your grandchildren wonder, "What if I don't like the job or career for which I am being trained? What if I'm not very good at it? What if I am bored to tears? What if my parents and peers don't approve?" The questions go on and on, and the more emerging adults think about them, the more confused and indecisive we may become.

Ideally everyone would be able to find a lucrative job that is fulfilling and meaningful. Unfortunately, for emerging adults with a relative lack of knowledge and experience, these jobs are hard to attain. Insofar as there are choices in the employment search these days, two job types seem to exist: financially rewarding jobs and fulfilling jobs. When evaluating these job types and the consequences and nuances associated with them, grandparents can provide insight into how their career choices affected their lives. Some grandparents worked jobs that provided a good income but did little to satisfy. Others worked fulfilling jobs with little financial remuneration. The breadth of your knowledge allows you to teach your grandchildren about the importance of each experience.

During our times of exploration, you can teach us how to be content. We may need to work whatever job we can get just because we need the money. We need to learn how to be satisfied during these times, even if little satisfaction comes from the work we do. Many of you have lived through lean times and times of plenty, and know that true happiness is not determined by the balance of a bank account. You can testify with the apostle Paul, "I have learned to be content whatever the circumstances. I know what it is to be in need, and I know what it is to have plenty. I have learned the secret of being content in any and every situation, whether well fed or hungry, whether living in plenty or in want. I can do everything through him who gives me strength" (Philippians

4:11–13 NIV). Grandparents give us a perspective that helps us be content on whichever path we find ourselves.

## Explorations in Worldview

A worldview is a collection of beliefs that form a comprehensive theory of the world and our place in it. Worldviews are shaped by a variety of factors, including religion, morality, and justice. For Christians, the Bible is the source of these beliefs. Many emerging adults have already or are in the process of questioning beliefs. We are trying to decide if we still believe what we grew up learning. New experiences, new knowledge, and new influences all compel us to wonder if what we always held to be true is in fact the Truth.

This process of questioning is not necessarily an outright rejection of the worldview of our parents or grandparents, but a need to create some distance and autonomy. We want to work out our beliefs for ourselves. It may be alarming for grandparents that grandchildren could end up believing something different than they do. Many grandparents are concerned for the spiritual well-being of their grandchildren and want grandchildren to share their faith. Love us anyway, always.

Morality is often derived from religious beliefs, but morality can take shape outside of these traditions as well. How we treat the people around us, how we handle difficult circumstances, and how we define our values are all moral decisions. We need moral behavior to be modeled for us, especially by our grandparents. You hold a special place in our eyes, and it is often easier to look up to you than our parents, whose flaws we know all too well. Whether we hold the same religious beliefs, your morality is bound to have a profound effect on us as we try to navigate our way through the difficulties we face every day.

Your grandchildren's experiences and influences may lead to changes in them. Because of their travels or new city of residence, they may speak differently, eat different food, and adopt a culture or tradition different from their family's. They may not eat Grandma's spaetzle with much gusto, and there is a good chance they will vote differently than you will. This may be disheartening or even downright hurtful. When they share what they are learning, understand that they are not snubbing your values, but rather being honest about their explorations because they feel comfortable in their relationship with you. The greatest gift you can give them is the knowledge of your unconditional love, no matter their political affiliation or favorite sports team.

## Explorations in Identity

Identity is still evolving for emerging adults. We are no longer the children our parents raised, nor are we the adults we will become. How we define ourselves is an exercise in balancing influences—friends, culture, heritage, and traditions. However, often we explore our identity on our own, without the daily companionship of our families.

As discussed in chapter 1, grandparents act as family historians and keepers of customs. In a time of questioning and instability, we need our family to anchor us. Friends are very important to us, and often act as our sounding boards and support systems, but our friends are rarely much wiser than we are.

Grandparents know their grandchildren—where we came from, how we were raised, the values that have been instilled in us—and this gives you invaluable clout to guide us through identity crises. These crises take on many forms: *I don't know what career I should pursue; I always thought I wanted children but now I'm not so sure; I don't know if I can handle living in the same city as my parents.* They deal with the fundamental question we are trying to answer—who am I?

Undoubtedly you will be disappointed in us sometimes (or often). Sometimes you will be so disappointed you will want to cry. We hope to give you a reason to cry proud tears as well. But tears or no tears, we need you to believe in us. We need you to anchor us. Remind us of where we came from and where we want to go. Remind us where you came from and how you got where you are. You provide a connection to the past and a glimpse into what we may someday accomplish in the future. Your faith, your breadth of experience, your values, all serve as testimony to the fact that a fulfilling, meaningful life can be found in many ways.

## Navigating a Way Forward

In order to navigate the complicated world ahead of us, many emerging adults will embark on various paths of exploration. We will find and fall out of love, find jobs and quit them quickly, reject and embrace various worldviews, and try to figure out—amidst all of this—who we are. Arnett aptly describes the potential pitfalls of emerging adulthood:

> Explorations in love sometimes result in disappointment, disillusionment, or rejection. Explorations in work sometimes result in a failure to achieve the occupation most desired or in an inability to find work that is satisfying and fulfilling. Explorations in worldviews

sometimes lead to rejection of childhood beliefs without the construction of anything more compelling in their place.

As grandparents, you have the opportunity to guide us through decisions and identity formation. We need the support, guidance, wisdom, and confidence of our grandparents. Grandchildren need coaches and cheerleaders in our school years, but we need them now too. We need them so we can be confident, have good relationships, get jobs, and define our place in the world. As emerging adults, we may need our grandparents now more than ever.

Grandchildren who are emerging adults need creative grandparents who are involved in their lives. These grandparents will not be disappointed. Their lives will be deeply enriched by these grandchildren as they become their friends. Friends are there for one another when needed. Friends are companions in adventure. Friends are present in times of celebration. Friends are ready to help in times of sadness. Friends accept one another. Becoming friends with your emerging adult grandchildren may be one of the best decisions of your life!

As friends, the scope of activities grandparents and their grandchildren can enjoy together is broad. Maya is twenty-two and loves to shop for jewelry with her grandmother. Nick and his grandfather love watching horror movies together. Find something you can both enjoy and do it. So many of us, young and old, are afraid to try new things. Emerging adults are fortunate in this regard: we are forced into newness daily. Learn from us and be open to new experiences. Your relationships with your grandkids will be enriched by your willingness to try new things.

## 25 Creative Things to Do with Your Emerging Adult Grandchildren

1. Go shopping at a major mall in a large city like Chicago or New York.
2. Take a trip to Boston and walk the Freedom Trail.
3. Travel together to the birthplace of *your* grandparents to learn about their roots.
4. Take a college course to learn what your grandchild is learning.
5. Visit their college campus. Have them give you a tour with a special dinner afterward at their favorite restaurant.
6. Take a nostalgic trip to the zoo they visited when they were young.
7. Have them interview you regarding your life story.
8. Join a local choir or orchestra together.
9. Join a book club together.
10. Do a landscaping or remodeling project for a friend or family member.
11. Go deep sea fishing.
12. Plan a menu and cook a special dinner together, and then deliver it to a person in need.
13. Go snorkeling.
14. Visit a presidential museum.
15. Go on a riverboat cruise.
16. Attend a NASCAR or dirt track race.
17. Attend an art festival or visit an art museum.
18. Visit a used-book store.
19. Tour a manufacturing plant.
20. Visit a car museum.

21. Scrapbook together.
22. Go skydiving.
23. Visit Civil War sites like Gettysburg.
24. Attend a Broadway play or musical theater.
25. Plan a Super Bowl party together.

## CHAPTER 6

# Involved but Not Interfering

Marcia is feeling pretty good about herself. On her own initiative she went to the local cycle shop and picked out a beautiful bright pink bicycle for her five-year-old granddaughter, Beka. It wasn't easy deciding which bike to purchase. Not just any bicycle would do. Beka was special, vivacious, and full of love and kinetic energy. Searching for a bike that matched Beka's personality was a long and exhaustive task. At last Marcia found it, complete with streamers and a picture of a golden-haired girl on the bar. Marcia didn't hesitate. She pulled out her credit card and took the bike home that day, lugging it to her car with help from the man who sold it to her.

True, Beka already had a bike, but Marcia wanted Beka to have a nicer one—one that didn't have a flat tire, a torn seat, and a rusty chain. Beka had been asking her mom for a new bike, but she was told she didn't need a new one, the old one worked just fine, and besides, bikes were expensive. Marcia knew that she would be Beka's hero for buying the bike. So, on a bright Saturday in May, Marcia presented her surprised and thrilled granddaughter with her new bicycle. The huge smile and big bear hug were well worth the time, energy, and $229 she had spent. Grandma returned home glowing, a hero to her granddaughter.

Dorie, Marcia's daughter, was not thrilled. Being a single mom was tough. Money had been tight since the divorce. Her job barely provided food, clothes, and a roof over her and her two daughters' heads. Extras like a new bike were not possible. Beka had been asking for a bike all spring. Dorie really wished that she could afford it, but the money just wasn't available. Trying to explain that to Beka wasn't easy. In the end Beka had sulked off to her room, dragging her feet and muttering about how when she was a mom, she wouldn't be so mean.

Then Grandma came riding to the rescue, like the cavalry in an old John Wayne movie. Just as Beka was beginning to understand that her bike could be fixed for a few dollars, that she didn't need all kinds of new things, that earning money for food and paying the bills were part of real life, in comes Grandma. Dorie was angry just thinking about it. How could her mother have spent $229 for a new bike that Beka didn't need when Dorie was worried about paying the electric bill? Why didn't she ask first? Dorie would have told her that she was trying to help Beka learn the value of money. It was important for her to understand that $229 is a lot of money— money that must be earned, money that could be spent on more important things.

To Dorie, this was yet another example of her mother's interference. Ever since the divorce, under the guise of helping the family through a tough time, her mom had been trying to parent her children. She bought them presents all the time, promised them a trip to Disneyland that Dorie could never afford, and took them frequently for ice cream—all without asking her. Dorie was frustrated and hurt. These were her girls, and she was losing them to her own mother. Whenever Mom had to say no, Grandma said yes. Now Beka and Lisa didn't even bother asking Mom. They bypassed her and went right to the source of the bounty, Grandma. And Grandma Marcia rarely said no.

The line between being an involved, creative grandparent and interfering with the parenting of your grandchildren is easily crossed. As with Marcia and Dorie, the perceptions of the grandparents and parents often differ. Grandma thought she was helping out, being a good grandparent, giving her granddaughters things their mother could not afford in their present circumstances. Mom saw it as an intrusion into her territory as a parent. She felt threatened and angry.

In this chapter we will examine the issue of involvement versus interference. How can grandparents be creatively involved in the lives of their grandchildren without interfering with their parenting? To answer this question, we will look at the issues of discipline, expectations, lifestyle, and spoiling as they relate to interference and involvement. We will also suggest clear guidelines for grandparents who are eager to know where the invisible line between involvement and interference lies.

## Discipline: Not Your Problem!

Questions about disciplining children can provoke deep differences of opinion between parents and grandparents.

This issue presents a strong temptation for grandparents to move beyond involvement to interference. It can be extremely painful for us to watch our children discipline our grandchildren. They have different rules to govern discipline than we did. When we raised children, spanking was commonplace. The maxim was: "Spare the rod, spoil the child." Today physical punishment has fallen into disrepute among child development experts. Our children, raised under corporal punishment, find themselves in the middle. On the one side are their parents, making dire predictions about alcohol and drug abuse in children who grow up without "proper guidance." By "proper guidance," of course, grandparents usually mean spanking. On the other side of the issue are the parenting professionals, who predict equally horrible consequences for children who are spanked regularly.

As grandparents, we say things like, "If you ever talked like that to me when you were a kid, I would have taught you a thing or two." "Remember what I always told you, Son, 'I brought you into this world and I can take you out.'" "I tell you what, you had respect for me, not like that disrespectful kid of yours." If we feel that our children are too permissive in their parenting style, we may not be shy about letting them know it. Our motives are pure. We want our grandchildren to grow up to be terrific human beings. But we think our way is the only way to achieve that.

The issue could also be deeper and more malignant. We may be trying to control our grown children. We may be much more interested in getting them to do our thing than the right thing. It feels like a slap in the face, like a renunciation of our methods, when our child's parenting style differs from ours. This is especially true if they appear to be successful. We are hurt and a little angry; they feel rejected and unappreciated. One sad grandparent expressed his feelings this way: "Was I such a horrible parent, spanking my children? They turned out all right. But now, he acts as if his children are too precious to spank. I bet my son thinks I was too hard on him. But I did my best. Why can't he do it the way he was brought up?" This grandparent is afraid that his children resent their childhood, which makes him question his own parenting. In his insecurity, he may become even more determined to prove that his way is the right way.

Sometimes we make our disapproval known in no uncertain terms to our grandchildren. Huge mistake! "Johnny, your mom and dad sure let you get away with a lot more than I ever would. Why, if you were my son, I'd let you know who was boss. I'm not your dad, and you can't get away with that stuff when you are with me." If we feel that our children should be tougher on their children, we release a big sigh and mutter under our breath, just loud enough for everyone to hear, "I guess the times have changed, but I wonder . . ."

The other side of the discipline debate is that sometimes we feel that our child is being too hard on our grandchildren. The urge is to jump into the middle of the fray and act as the family referee. This vote of no confidence is a sure way to enrage your children and confuse your grandchildren.

On occasion it may be proper and even necessary to intervene on your grandchildren's behalf. In instances of physical or sexual abuse, for example, grandparents not only have a right but also a responsibility to act in the best interests of the children to remove them from danger. They may even have to report their own children to the proper authorities.

For most grandparents, however, the issue is not abuse. Instead, it is a parent raising her voice, losing her temper, and punishing harshly rather than using appropriate discipline. As grandparents, we need to remember that we are not full-time members of the household. We can't know what has gone on before. If Jill has missed her curfew six straight weekends in a row and we only catch Mom losing it on the sixth weekend, we are not seeing the whole picture.

Remember, grandparents are a step removed from the parenting process. Parents are responsible to look at their long-term goals for their children. They want them to become well functioning, valuable members of society. Of course, grandparents want no less for their grandchildren, but their position allows them to work toward a different set of goals: a loving look, a happy face, an assuring hug, a bright smile, and words that say "I love you, Grandma." But the look of love for Grandma or the bright smile for Grandpa does not come through discipline. The short-term pain brought into our grandchildren's lives by their parents' discipline hurts us too. Even though we know in our heads that discipline in the long term is beneficial, our hearts betray us and we move in to interfere and prevent the short-term pain. This is understandable. But it's also understandable when our children do not serenely let us interfere with their parenting.

We experienced this a few years ago. I had a ski trip lined up with Erin and Jay. I love these times together and always look forward to them. The day before the trip I was in the garage packing the car with skis, boots, poles, and all the layers of clothing required for a late-winter day outdoors in Michigan. Then I got a call; Erin and her father, Jack, were having a disagreement. Erin was told if she continued to talk back to her father, then she would not be able to go on the ski trip. Erin is a strong, verbal, persistent person and continued the argument even though her dad said the conversation was over. Well, Jack, needing to stick to his word and show Erin what the consequences for bad behavior were, took away the ski trip.

Erin called in tears. I had to bite my tongue not to say to Jack, "You are punishing me as well as Erin. All she did was talk back to you—something you often did to me when you were a teenager. Can't you issue another punishment so she can still go? This seems too harsh for the crime." But instead I told Erin that I was sorry she wouldn't be going. I went skiing with Jay, without his sister. I overcame my disappointment, had a great time with Jay, and survived without being guilty of interference. Erin did not miss another ski trip because of her temper.

Our children can find themselves between the proverbial immovable object (us) and the irresistible force (their parental responsibility). Interfering with the parenting of our grandchildren may make us feel more in control or more important, but it only damages our fragile relations with our children and makes their job more difficult. When we step in, we send a very loud message that our child is not capable of parenting on his own. And the parents are not the only ones who receive this message. Our grandchildren soon observe the contempt we show toward their parents. This makes discipline all the more difficult. Usually our stated goal is to help our children be better parents. Ironically, our interference actually sabotages our children's effectiveness.

Angie is sixteen. By most standards, she is a good kid. She does well in school, doesn't do drugs, and doesn't drink.

Angie does have a long-term relationship with her boyfriend that sometimes irritates her parents, especially when she chooses to be with her boyfriend rather than with the family. He's a nice kid, but they think Angie is too young to be dating so seriously. Angie is allowed to see her boyfriend on weekends and one night during the week. Her parents, Valerie and Doug, have just discovered that she has been sneaking out to see him after they go to bed on weeknights. They are angry and afraid about what this could mean. It could mean they're sexually involved; it could mean Angie is lying about other things as well.

The situation came to a head when Valerie's parents came to town for a weeklong visit. Valerie caught Angie crawling back into her room through the window one night, and the ensuing argument woke Grandma. She put on her old housecoat and went to investigate the cause of the midnight ruckus. When Grandma heard the story, she laughed out loud and said to Valerie, "Remember when you used to sneak out of the house to be with Tommy Herman? I knew the whole time what you were doing, but I never said a word. Now, why don't you just let Angie get to sleep and leave her alone?" Valerie was furious. She felt it was right to ground Angie for a month, and now Angie was laughing at her with Grandma. Valerie had lost control of the situation. Her mother had ruined her credibility with Angie, not by disclosing her youthful foibles, but by treating Valerie's indignation and anger as unimportant. Valerie knew that Grandma's reaction would be used as ammunition in their next battle over boyfriends.

Angie's grandmother had stepped beyond involvement to interference. Yet to this day she tells that story with pride. She really thinks the embarrassed look that came over her daughter's face was funny, and she is convinced that she saved Angie from a grave injustice. Last Christmas, Grandma told the story to the entire family, much to the delight of almost everyone present. She thought Valerie was being a little too dramatic when she stomped out of the room, followed by the laughter of the family. This grandmother had not learned how to keep from interfering with parental discipline.

The rule is simple: Discipline is not our problem. Whenever we offer unsolicited advice on our children's disciplinary actions, we have overstepped our bounds. Bite your tongue. Your children are going to make mistakes. Mine do too, at least by my standards. Our children need to learn on their own, just as we did.

If you force your advice and wisdom on your children, they will resent it, and you. But if you give your children the freedom to discipline as they see fit without hounding them into doing it your way, they may even come to you for the very advice that you want so dearly to give them. Not long ago, my son asked me, "Dad, do you think I'm too hard on my children?" Jack was concerned that his discipline, although rarely corporal, was too harsh. He wondered if he was expecting too much from his kids. It was reassuring and affirming for him when I was able to say, "No, Jack. You're doing a great job. I think you're a terrific dad." If Judy and I had tried to force him to follow our thinking on discipline, or made him look foolish in front of his children, he may never have given us the opportunity to comment on his parenting and encourage him.

Don't push your children away. Discipline is not your problem. Any attempt to make it your responsibility without being asked will produce pain and hard feelings.

## Expectations: Too High or Too Low?

Bill did not finish high school. Although he is still not retired at the age of sixty-five, he used to work ten- to twelve-hour days to scratch out a living for his wife and two sons. Bill wanted something better than the steel mills for his boys, so he was tough on them, especially when it came to schoolwork. They were expected to do well in school, because Bill wanted his sons to go to college. His lifelong dream, the one that got him up at five o'clock every morning, was that they would have a better life than him. They were bright boys, and they loved their father. They did what they were told. Both of Bill's sons went on to medical school. One became a surgeon, the other an anesthesiologist. Both of Bill's boys had sons of their own.

But now Bill is angry. Joseph, his oldest grandson, has just reluctantly shown Grandpa his report card. He had earned two Bs, three Cs, and a D. Grandpa was furious. He walked over to his son and asked, "Did you see that boy's horrible report card? He should be grounded. Did you tell him he has to do better next time?"

"Dad, I talked to Joe, and he really tried his best. He is not a student, and he probably never will be. I don't really care what grades he gets as long as he does his best."

"Does his best?" Grandpa thundered. "It's obvious that he's just lazy. He's fifteen and you treat him like he's still a baby. I'm telling you, he isn't going to amount to anything if you don't get tougher on him and make him grow up."

Bill angered his son and his daughter-in-law by interfering with their parenting. But that's not all. He nearly broke his grandson's heart, because Joseph heard his Grandpa's tirade. Bill insists that he didn't step over the line. He blames his son for not expecting enough from Joseph.

Our ideals as grandparents can cause us to interfere in the parenting of our grandchildren. We look for them to complete developmental tasks, such as walking and talking, early. We have high standards for their behavior. We have special dreams for their future. We know what kind of people we want them to grow up to be, and what we think they should do with their lives.

These expectations are often our little secret. We don't let anyone in on them. They are hidden from view, crystallize slowly, and appear without our making a conscious effort to form them. Once in place, however, they are a powerful force in our grandparenting.

Nothing is wrong with having high ideals for your grandchildren. That's natural. Problems occur when our hopes become unreasonable and our expectations too rigid. We have two grandchildren who were verbal very early, and two who did not talk clearly until later. By coincidence, it was the first grandchild who spoke early and clearly. We were delighted to listen to her jabber around the house. At two years of age, Lauren recited all of *The Night Before Christmas*. We couldn't believe it! We were convinced that she was the smartest little girl in the world. Then Erin came along, and at three she was talking like a teenager. We decided that we had the two smartest grandchildren in the world. Their verbal skills created within us the expectation that all of our grandchildren would develop early. We were wrong. As toddlers, Jay and Elena were not as verbal as Lauren and Erin. Our expectations were out of line with reality. Some children simply talk earlier than others, and it has little or nothing to do with intelligence.

Many grandparents spend a lot of time bragging about their grandchildren. It's their favorite pastime. Sometimes these sessions become competitive.

"My grandson walked at eleven months. I heard that your grandson didn't walk until he was thirteen months old. What was wrong with him?"

"Well, he didn't walk until thirteen months but he knew *Hamlet* by heart when he was three."

"My granddaughter walked out of the womb quoting the Bible."

You get the idea. These exchanges between grandparents and friends create developmental expectations that no child could live up to. So we respond by pushing the parents. We ask our children if they have considered a speech therapist because in our minds, two-year-olds who don't talk well are already behind. We try to get the children to walk to us at eight months of age. We nag our child about any marginal lack of development. We worry about whether our grandchildren are being potty-trained soon enough, and if they wet the bed we worry that they will do so forever. We're concerned that our daughters and daughters-in-law are nursing their babies too long. If the children aren't on a schedule, we worry, and if they suck their thumb after age two, we panic.

If we kept our expectations to ourselves, we would probably be okay. But most of us feel the need to share our concerns with our children, and for some reason we share them repeatedly and often. In the process we create frustration and anger. We shame our children, and we make them embarrassed for their children. What is even worse, we are putting enormous weight on tiny shoulders.

Being toilet-trained at twelve, eighteen, or twenty-four months does not determine whether our grandchildren are going to be successful in life. I'm sure there are corporate executives who didn't know *The Night Before Christmas* at two years of age and I am sure there are college graduates who sucked their thumbs in kindergarten.

Grandparents also have high expectations for behavior. One grandfather refused to take his children out to dinner because they were young, wiggly, and loud. He was embarrassed by toddlers who did not live up to his lofty expectations. Little children cannot sit quietly for very long, and you can't punish toddlers for acting like toddlers. Yet we often hear grandparents in restaurants complaining to their children because their young grandchildren are not living up to their expectations. "Debbie, can't you keep the kids quiet? For crying out loud, everyone in the restaurant is looking at us. Now be quiet, Jason. Please be quiet . . ." Of course, it is at that point that Jason slides out of his high booster seat and takes off at full speed. Every time you express embarrassment at your grandchildren's behavior, you are communicating something essential to them about their unacceptability. Misbehaving is one thing; acting like a kid is another. Instead of spending your time being embarrassed and angry, do what you can to entertain them or choose a family restaurant next time. That's the creative, involved way to grandparent.

We want our teenage grandchildren to conform to adult standards of behavior. We expect them to act like "young gentlemen and ladies." This is not unreasonable, except that what we usually mean is, "Don't act like an American teenager." We're shocked when they slouch past us in torn jeans, a rap T-shirt, and sporting several earrings. "Jill, what is Bobby wearing? I can't believe you let him dress like that. I would never have let my kids out of the house looking like that."

Judy's mother used to wonder if my son Jack respected Judy and me because of the way he spoke to us. When Jack was about thirteen he called me Pops. Once, in his grandmother's presence, he made fun of my receding hairline by calling me Baldy. His grandma was aghast that we would let our children speak to us that way: "Judy, don't you think that's a funny way for him to talk to Jerry?" Judy, who knew the deep bond that Jack and I share, said no. She thought it was a sign of a good relationship that Jack would kid me like that. Still Grandma persisted. "But if anyone heard him talk to Jerry like that, what would they think?" Grandma was missing the point. She was interfering in our parenting. What she was really saying was, "You are not doing a good enough job raising your son. You are not teaching him to respect you. His behavior does not live up to my expectations." Today, Judy and I smile as we now hear Jack's son, Jay, call him Pops and tease him.

Perhaps we are most concerned about the future of our grandchildren. Because we want the best for them (and us), we develop expectations that suffocate our children and our grandchildren. You met Bill a few pages back. Bill is not a lousy grandfather. But his expectations for his grandchildren are causing him to interfere loudly and obnoxiously. Is Bill wrong to want the best for his grandchildren? Of course not. But Bill steps over the line in the way he communicates his ideals. He has developed rigid and unrealistic expectations. His grandchildren will never be able to measure up to them. What is Bill going to do if his oldest grandson decides he wants to pick raspberries for a living? Is he going to disown him? Will he stay angry at the parents indefinitely? Bill's expectations and his interference will inevitably limit his grandparenting opportunities. That would be the real tragedy, not a grandson who picks raspberries.

Our children will resent our intrusion if we force our expectations onto their parenting. It drives a wedge into our relationship with our children and our grandchildren. The guideline for dealing with your ideals is this: Don't lock your children and grandchildren into your expectations. Let them grow and develop into the human beings God wants them to be, with their own unique gifts, skills, and personalities combining to make a wonderful creation.

## Lifestyles: Different Isn't Wrong

Josie walks past Grandma Rose with her head bouncing and her body swaying. Grandma cannot ignore the music coming from Josie's iPod. The lyrics sound trashy to Grandma. Josie is wearing a tight, short skirt and a sheer blouse with a skimpy tank top underneath. "Josie, Josie, JOSIE!"

"Yes, Gram?"

"You're not going out like that are you?"

Josie laughs. She loves grandma and treasures spending time with her, but her grandmother is just so, well . . . old. "Sure, Grandma. It's not like I'm naked or anything. See ya later."

Rose shook her head. She wondered if she should bring it up to her children. Josie seems so unsupervised. Her parents are too relaxed about her lifestyle. Grandma Rose had a horrible feeling that Josie and her boyfriend were . . . well, you know, "doing it." She decided that the issue was too important to ignore, so she marched into her daughter's office. "Barbra, did you see what Josie had on? I'm sorry, but she looks like a, a . . . well, I can't even say it, but you know what I mean. And the music she listens to day and night is just plain immoral. Did I bring you up so badly that you ignore what your children are doing?"

Lifestyle differences can be sources of deep irritation between parents and grandparents. Both are afraid the child is going off the deep end. The parent doesn't want to be reminded of this fear. The grandparent may feel that the parent has somehow overlooked the orange spiked hair her teenage daughter is currently sporting. She feels the need to point it out, just in case. The result of this kind of interference is friction and guilt. The parents may not be happy about the lifestyles of their children, but they have already decided that it's best not to try to change it. By harping on it, grandparents escape feeling guilty for not taking some kind of action. Once again, this can be devastating. Angry parents can reduce our access to those grandchildren we love so dearly and want to see, even if they do have orange hair.

An even more difficult situation arises when grandparents take issue with the lifestyle of the parent. One grandmother is exceedingly tidy. Well, tidy might be understating the case. The woman is positively eccentric about cleanliness. Her children, probably out of reaction to growing up in a surgically sterile environment, are not as clean. One of them is positively untidy. No, let's tell the truth. This guy is sloppy. And his wife accentuates, rather than alleviates, that quality in him.

Following the birth of her first grandchild, Grandma came to help take care of the baby. Her son and his wife were apprehensive. They felt Grandma might have a few negative things to say about their laid-back way of life. They were wrong. She had *many* negative things to say about their life-style. "I can't believe you are going to raise a baby in a place like this. You haven't scrubbed the floor in months, your couch is covered with dog hair, and your refrigerator is growing things. The baby will probably get every disease known to humankind from the germs on your floor." Well, unsurprisingly, the son and his wife could only take so much. On the fourth day of what was to have been a ten-day visit, they ushered Grandma out the door and to the airport. They purchased a first-class ticket for her and, feeling relieved, watched her fly away.

Was Grandma right? Did her son need to be cleaner? I'm sure. Was she wrong in the way she handled it? You bet. Today they are still angry with one another. The baby did not get a terrible disease and the house is still a mess. It is very sad to see this relationship damaged because of dirt, which is not worth the trouble. The key phrase we must keep in mind when tempted to interfere with lifestyle is this: *It's their life, let them live it.*

We want the best for our children and grandchildren, and are convinced that we know exactly what is best for them. Chances are that we've got it figured out a lot more completely than they do. But they are human beings, and ultimately they are responsible for making their own way in the world. They are free to decide what kind of people they want to be. It's their life, let them live it. As much as we would like to, we cannot make lifestyle decisions for our grown children. I know all about the urge to interfere. I feel it, and I have to fight it myself. But the rule is a good one. If we spend our time harping on nonessential things like clothing and hair or a clean house our children and grandchildren will be deaf to us when we need to speak to them about matters of importance.

## Spoiling: When Is Enough, Enough?

The most frequent complaint about grandparents is that they spoil their grandchildren. Many grandparents tend to laugh it off. They feel or say aloud that a grandparent's job is to spoil their grandchildren. Often, we mean that we want to be free to give our grandchildren things we didn't give our children. But our son or daughter does not see it in such a favorable light. They see us as spoiling their children by giving them too much or giving them gifts that are too expensive.

This issue isn't really between you and your children. The real issue, although obscured by bickering and hurt feelings, is delayed gratification. Social scientists and child psychologists are pointing toward a new and disturbing trend in the personalities of today's young people. Children seem incapable of waiting for things. They want it all, they want it now, and they want it without sacrifice. M. Scott Peck, in *The Road Less Traveled,* pointed to this phenomenon as "one of the roots of the selfishness and unhappiness of Americans."

Our grandchildren are being brought up in a world where sensuality is prominent and pleasure is the reigning pursuit. By *sensuality* I'm not speaking of sexuality, although sexuality is part of it. I'm speaking of indulging our senses, living at the mercy of the whims or our sensory feelings and emotions. That is the way of life for many of our grandchildren.

When Lauren was seven years old, she looked around her neighborhood and saw what was going on. She saw what her friends were buying, wearing, and owning. And she wanted that. All of it. That year, the grade-school rage was roller blades. They are very fast, very fun, very popular, and can be very expensive. So Lauren begged her father for roller blades.

"Dad, please. Dad, I can't go outside if I don't have roller blades. Please . . ." Seven-year-olds have a way of putting on incredible pressure when they want something and feel they are being denied unfairly.

Her father was adamant. "Lauren, last year you had to have roller skates. This winter it was ice skates. I bought them for you. If you want roller blades you will have to save your allowance and buy them with your own money."

"But, Dad, I need them now! Can't you just charge them? I'll pay you back later. I promise I'll never ask for anything again."

I was with Lauren during her quest for roller blades. We hadn't been together three minutes when she asked me if we could go to the store and get roller blades. Judy and I love to buy things for our grandchildren. We love the look in their eyes when we bring a new gift to them and they just explode with joy. But this time I said no to Lauren. I thought that there might be more to the story and refused to buy the roller blades until I talked to Jon and Lynn. Good thing I resisted Lauren's appeal! When I conferred with Jon, he told me the story.

"Dad, Lauren was crying and throwing a fit because I wouldn't buy her roller blades. I told her she had to save up her own money and pay for them herself. She was almost out of control when I asked her to look at my shoes. I said, 'Lauren, how do my shoes look to you?' She said they looked terrible. I asked if she thought I should get new ones. She thought that, yeah, the time had definitely come for new shoes. Then I looked in her eyes and asked how much new shoes would cost. She thought that I could probably buy them for about forty-five dollars. Then I asked, 'Lauren, why haven't I bought new shoes?' She haltingly answered, 'Because you don't have the money?' I smiled and nodded my head and asked her why I wasn't buying roller blades. 'Because you don't have the money,' was the slow response.

"Dad, if you had bought her those roller blades, it would have messed up what I'm trying to do with Lauren. She thinks everything is hers for the taking right now. And I'm trying to teach her that getting things comes through hard work, through doing what you don't always want to do. Thanks for not interfering."

I learned a lot as I listened to that story. I realized, probably for the first time, that the key issue isn't spoiling. It is helping our children teach their children to become responsible adults. Responsible adults know how to delay gratification. Most parents establish long-term goals for their children. You and I are usually thinking short-term when we seek love and hugs from our grandchildren. We don't have to be as tough. And that's all right, as long as we don't compromise what our children are trying to accomplish.

"'Everything is permissible'—but not everything is beneficial. 'Everything is permissible'—but not everything is constructive. Nobody should seek his own good, but the good of others" (1 Corinthians 10:23–24 NIV). The apostle Paul's point is well taken by creative grandparents. Spoiling is not constructive, it is not beneficial, and ultimately it is not for the good of others. Loving our grandchildren means that sometimes we forego the fleeting pleasure of seeing them light up when we bring them a new treasure. We must be willing to help build character. Creative grandparents can help their grandchildren build character by refusing to interfere in matters of discipline, expectations, lifestyle, and spoiling.

## Involvement versus Interference

All involved, creative grandparents will step over the line at times and interfere. Don't think you are a bad grandparent if you are accused of interfering. You are not intentionally causing problems. You merely went too far with your involvement.

Sometimes the line between involvement and interference is not clear. What we may consider involved, creative grandparenting may look like interfering to our children. How can we avoid crossing the line? Keep the following realities in mind.

*Responsibility rests with the parents.* This is what makes grandparenting so wonderful. We are not responsible for outcomes. This is the parents' job, and we must allow them to do that job in the way that seems right to them. Most of the time parents will do just fine, without grandparents' interference.

*Authority rests with the parents.* With responsibility comes authority. Don't usurp parents' authority. Usurping the parents' authority will only make matters worse for everyone involved—you, your children, and your grandchildren. The parents' authority comes from God, not us. He gives parents the authority and responsibility to raise children appropriately. Don't try to steal a role that God has designated for your children.

*Assumptions can be harmful.* Don't assume; ask first. As creative grandparents become more sensitive to their own desire to interfere, certain actions will become questionable to us. We will sense the need to talk to our children before making a purchase or speaking our mind or commenting on the plans and expectations of the parents for our grandchildren. We avoid doing damage by asking first.

*Context is important.* You may not be hearing the whole story or seeing the complete picture. Sometimes our grandchildren omit important facts when asking us to participate in an activity or purchase an item for them. We need to get the whole story from parents before taking action or sharing our opinions.

*Reconciliation is imperative.* When our children accuse us of interfering with their plans and expectations for our grandchildren, we must not be defensive. Instead quickly admit the mistake, agree with the parents, ask for forgiveness, and promise not to repeat the action again. Acknowledge your faults and pursue peace. "If it is possible, as far as it depends on you, live at peace with everyone" (Romans 12:18 NIV).

Interference is not the end of the world. However, it is serious. Time to back off and draw the line in a different place. The best way to know we are interfering is to listen to our children. They will be the first to notice. As soon as our interference is brought to our attention, we need to pull back. Don't sabotage your opportunities to be with your grandchildren by insisting on your right to interfere.

Don't go to the other extreme of noninvolvement either. Sometimes we feel hurt, move away, and severely limit our involvement. Our children are not asking us to stop our involvement, only our interference. Find the parents' comfort level and live with it.

Be thankful for every moment you can spend with your grandchildren. Influence your grandchildren toward good and toward God while you can. Stay involved, but clearly distinguish between involvement and interference. Creative grandparents are ever learning to be the very best they can be. Many times our children will be our best teachers. Wise grandparents will listen to their teachers and be involved without interfering.

## CHAPTER 7

# In Difficult Times

It was one of those calls every parent dreads—the stuff of sleepless nights and agonizing days. "Dad, this is Rebecca. I'm over at Patty's house. You guys need to come over right away."

For Pam and Mike, the drive down the familiar road to their daughter Patty's house seemed endless. They couldn't help but wonder what was happening. Was one of their daughters sick? Or could it be that their four-month-old grandson Jason, the joy of their lives, had suddenly become ill? When they walked through the door of their oldest daughter's home, Pam caught her breath. It was obvious that their two daughters had been crying. Pam's eyes scanned the room, searching for Jason's bassinet. Relief at seeing him sleeping peacefully in the corner overwhelmed her. She was not aware how concerned she had been. But what was wrong?

Rebecca spoke quietly. "Patty, maybe you'd better tell them yourself."

"Tell us. What's wrong? We're worried sick. We thought something had happened to Jason."

Patty tried to speak, but her voice broke. Finally she blurted out, "Mom, Dad, I can't believe this is happening to me." The words were gushing now, like water. "James came home from work Friday and he said . . . he said . . . he's been seeing someone else."

"What do you mean? Was he telling you that he's having an affair?"

"Yes! And, oh, Dad, he's been seeing her for more than a year. I don't know what to do. He wants a divorce. This isn't happening. It can't be! Mom, he loves me. At least he is supposed to. But the whole time I was pregnant with Jason, he was sleeping with her." Patty's body shook.

Mike looked around. Rebecca was crying. He felt an air of unreality at being called away from a normal supper on a normal day and being told the kind of news that made his heart ache for his oldest daughter.

Mike glanced at his sleeping grandson. The infant was unaware of the hard turn his life had taken. Mike was not one to show his emotions, but he buried his face in his burly hands and cried. He wept for the hurt to his daughter. He wept for the uncertainty of his grandchild's future. He wept for the shattering of his own dreams.

It wasn't supposed to be this way. He and Pam had been good parents. They had raised their children in the church. They had instilled in them good values by teaching and example. His daughters had grown to be mature, attractive Christian women. They had married, purchased homes, borne children. Life was good. Everything seemed perfect—until this. Mike wondered how everyone would be affected now that his daughter's family appeared to be falling apart. Was reconciliation still possible? Was it too late? Life had taken a difficult turn indeed. It appeared that life would never be quite the same.

Mike and Pam's experience is all too common. Many families have experienced similar heartbreak. One moment the world is revolving on its axis and all is well; the next, it seems to have careened off course and is spinning wildly out of control.

In this chapter we will think together about how grandparents can be a help and resource during two common life crises their children may face: divorce and death of a family member. No one can ever really be ready for these kinds of catastrophic events. Sometimes we're afraid even to talk about them. But death occurs in every family and divorce is becoming more prevalent, even in Christian families. And if they do occur, creative, involved grandparents can be the difference between the family that handles the crisis successfully and the one that collapses under the strain and pressure. Grandparents can offer two things their family needs most: help and hope.

## Grandparenting during Divorce

With our society's divorce rate continuing to soar, many parents will have to watch at least one of their children go through the pain and trauma of divorce. Current divorce statistics tell us that between 35 and 40 percent of first marriages end in divorce. This affects couples in the church as well as those outside the church. Some researchers claim that the rate of divorce is the same for Christians as others.

Our purpose here is not to debate the rightness or wrongness of divorce from cultural or biblical perspectives. Rather, we are approaching divorce as a sad reality of life in the twenty-first century. We want to show grandparents how they can creatively and constructively be involved in the lives of their children and grandchildren if divorce does occur. We strongly believe that grandparents can be a powerful help and source of hope during this traumatic experience. Divorce can be one of the most stressful experiences for families. Writers on the subject of stress include divorce in a list of catastrophic events that happen to families.

When circumstances force you to grandparent during the divorce of one of your children, consider the following recommendations:

- Don't judge hastily.
- Make yourself and your resources available.
- Establish clear boundaries around your role as a grandparent.
- Maintain contact with both parents.

*Don't judge hastily.* As Mike sat in his daughter's living room, he was overwhelmed with anger. How could his son-in-law behave that way? How could he have so little concern for his infant son? How could he just throw his marriage away? Mike wanted to find James and settle the score. He had not felt this way since he became a Christian many years ago. Mike's voice was controlled, steely, even though a fire burned hot inside him. "Patty, where is your husband? Why isn't he here?" With a rising voice, revealing an obvious effort to control his rage, he continued. "Patty, I want to talk to him. Tell me where he is."

"Dad, he's at work. He didn't want to be here when I told you. Please don't do something rash. It will only make things worse."

Mike paced the room. Then Mike and Pam offered support to Patty and reassurance of their continued love. On the way home, they talked. Mike's anger was subsiding and rationality had returned. As he expressed his feelings, Pam kept saying the same thing over and over, "Mike, remember, we don't know everything that went on in that house. It's not fair to blame James for everything. Let's wait until we get the whole story."

Mike resisted her efforts to get him to see both sides. He loved his daughter. He found it difficult to believe that she might share some of the responsibility. After all, James was having the affair. Patty had always been faithful.

The truth, however, was that Mike and Pam had foreseen difficulties in their daughter's relationship from the beginning. The shock was not that Patty and James were so close to a divorce, but that he had betrayed her with another woman. Even so, Pam's point was sensible. She and Mike would be able to help even more if they refrained from rushing into judgment.

A year and a half later, Mike and Pam looked back at this difficult time. When asked, "What advice would you give to parents during the divorce of their children?" immediately and almost in unison they answered, "Don't be judgmental. It's almost impossible to avoid pinning the blame on someone, but you have to try."

Creative grandparents who want to be a force for good and a source of support during the marital difficulties of their children must continuously fight their own deeply ingrained loyalties. The natural tendency is to side immediately with our own flesh and blood. We direct all the anger we feel at the other person involved. Not only is this unfair, but it may disrupt or destroy our relationship with our grandchildren.

Consider Marcy, whose grandchildren live with her divorced daughter. Marcy spends at least two afternoons a week with the children. She loves them and they love her. However, Marcy is deeply angry at her former son-in-law. Her daughter's divorce was unexpectedly bitter. The custody battle had been distasteful, with accusations and innuendo traded equally between combatants who, until recently, had been lovers and marriage partners. Every time she is with her grandchildren, Marcy cannot resist speaking against their father. She believes that the joint custody awarded by the court was a severe mistake, and she doesn't miss an opportunity to express her feelings to the children.

Marcy's rage and resentment have blinded her to the harm she is doing to her grandchildren. She is putting them into a position where they have to choose whom they are going to love, their father or their mother. Her grandchildren, only four and six, do not like her to watch them anymore. The anguish she causes in their half-formed psyches is too much for them. They love their mother *and* their father, and they still don't understand why Mom and Dad can't live together anymore. Grandma Marcy is making it even tougher on them to adjust and survive.

During the pain of divorce, everything in us cries out to make a snap judgment in defense of our children. We want to protect them, to justify their actions. But divorce is rarely a one-way street. Even in a situation that seems one-sided, such as an extramarital affair, the real difficulties often remain hidden. Most of the time an affair is a symptom of deeper issues, not the root cause. This is not to minimize the offense. But we must guard against becoming judge, jury, and executioner. At stake are things far more important than our personal sense of outrage: the possibility of reconciliation, the needs of our son or daughter, and the well-being of our grandchildren. For their sakes, and sometimes just to give the marriage a chance, we must learn to reserve judgment.

*Make yourself and your resources available.* During and after a divorce, we can provide a place of security and constant love for grandchildren who are afraid that they are going to lose one or both of their parents. Now that Mom or Dad has moved out, the children will wonder if the one who left has stopped loving them. They may be afraid that the parent they are living with will go away too, leaving them alone.

For children struggling with these feelings, creative grandparents can offer a reliable refuge during the stormy proceedings of the divorce and aftermath. Mom and Dad may be preoccupied and angry, but Grandma can quietly assure the children that she will love them and be there for them. Sometimes the parents each try to enlist the children to side with them in the divorce. The children are pulled by conflicting loyalties and confusing emotions. They do not need us to pressure them into taking sides; rather, they need us to be understanding and patient, providing quiet support and constant love.

We will also help them immensely if we maintain a degree of objectivity when they ask us about the divorce. This is how the conversation might go.

"Grandma, why did Mommy take us away from Daddy? Why can't he live with us anymore?"

"That, my dear granddaughter, is a grown-up question. You must be growing up. The answer to some questions is hard, Megan. I don't always understand what happened between your mom and dad either. But I do know this: They both love you very much. Your dad has promised that even though you aren't living together anymore, he will still see you often. Sometimes he will take you over to his house so you can stay with him."

"I know, Grandma, but why does Mom say mean things about Dad? Is he really that bad?"

"Honey, your mom is feeling hurt right now. Once she and your dad loved each other very much, but now they aren't so sure. This makes your mom very sad. When people are sad, sometimes they say bad things. Do you do that sometimes?"

"Yes, Grandma, I do. Will they stop loving me sometime too?"

"No, Megan, they will not. You are their daughter, and just like I will never stop loving your mom, she will never, ever stop loving you. And I know your dad feels the same way. And Megan, you will always be my special girl, even though you are growing up way too fast."

We can be a valuable resource to our children and grandchildren if we will listen more than talk. We must hear our children. We must hear their spouse. Of course, we must also listen to our grandchildren. We must let them tell us what they are thinking and feeling. Let them ask the difficult, "adult" questions. Let them express their fears. And when they do, we have to resist the temptation to provide simplistic responses or pat answers. Talk to them about the fact that both persons share responsibility for most divorces. Be open about the deep feelings of ambiguity and pain that accompany a divorce. Don't express your anger at your child or the marital partner to your grandchildren. Turn the energy the anger generates into being the best, wisest, most loving grandparent you can be. If you waste it on anger or bitterness, you will only add further turmoil to your grandchildren's already confused lives.

Mike and Pam were now faced with a difficult decision. After attempting to salvage her marriage by seeing a family counselor, their daughter decided to file for divorce. But the agreement said she had to be out of the house within thirty days, and she had no place to stay. Foreseeing this possibility, Mike and Pam had considered inviting their grown daughter and her infant son into their home. They weren't sure they were ready for that. Their lifestyle would have to change drastically. After being "on their own" for a number of years, they would be committing themselves to caring for a baby and their increasingly fragile daughter.

In the end, the decision was easy. There simply were no good alternatives. So they went to Patty together and asked her if she would temporarily move in with them. Relieved, Patty agreed: "Just for a few weeks, until I can afford an apartment." The few weeks stretched into months. Pam and Mike found themselves involved in their grandson's life to an extent they had never anticipated. But later they saw the time as a rewarding, fulfilling interlude in their lives.

During the stress of divorce, parents run low on two important resources: time and money. On an average, women's resources dip dramatically following a divorce, while men become responsible for child support. The result is a drain on everyone's financial resources. Although grandparents may not be affluent, they can be of help.

One grandparent we know realized that her daughter would never ask her for money, even in desperation. She did not want to be dependent upon her parents. She wanted to be a responsible adult, paying her own way. So this grandmother takes her grandchildren shopping and purchases clothes for them. Her daughter's muted protests are met with, "It's a grandmother's prerogative." Her daughter chooses to accept that, and she appreciates keeping her dignity while her children are getting the clothes they need.

One grandfather looked at the tires of his daughter's car and realized they needed replacing. It was dangerous to continue the drive the car with those tires. He knew that his daughter could not afford them now, in this time of family crisis, so he took the car to a tire shop and had new tires put on. On the way home, he noticed that the gas gauge was near empty so he pulled into a gas station and filled the car with gas. He then returned the car to its place in the driveway, without saying a word. He was just doing what he could to make his daughter's life a bit easier.

Another grandfather takes his divorced son and his grandson out to dinner once a week. He realizes that his son struggles with finances, and he knows that cooking day after day is not easy for him. So, once a week, they go out to eat as a family and Grandpa picks up the tab.

Creative grandparents will find many ways in which they can help their children or grandchildren when a divorce occurs. And they will find ways to do so without robbing their son or daughter of dignity. For example, one parent provided the security deposit for his daughter's apartment after she and her husband divorced and she had to give up their home. It was seven hundred dollars she just did not have. He let her know that he was doing it simply as an act of love, and she let him do it on that basis.

For your enjoyment and well-being as a parent, your involvement should be strictly voluntary. Choose to become involved and do what you can comfortably do. It's better to be willing to help your child than to feel obligated to do so. Don't try to meet your child's every need. If your child assumes that you will always come to the rescue, your involvement will become a burden to you rather than a blessing. You may become resentful and bitter instead of regarding this as an opportunity to love in a practical way. This is true of all kinds of help you may be in position to give, including child care.

Offering your time may be an even more important way to help than giving money over the long run. Divorcing parents are under a great deal of stress. Finding a new place to live, getting a job, meeting with lawyers, appearing in court, and negotiating the settlement may consume much of their time. The emotional drain is enormous. Creative grandparents will find ways to alleviate this strain.

Pam and Mike, for example, soon found themselves putting Jason to bed nearly every night. His mother, exhausted by stressful days of job hunting and personal adjustment, was relieved when Mom and Dad volunteered to give Jason his bath and dress him for bed. Patty greatly appreciated her mom's offer to watch Jason while she looked for work. She was also assured of her mom's assistance when she did find a job. When Patty needed a weekend away to sort out her thinking, do some healing, and look to the future, Pam and Mike volunteered to take care of Jason.

As creative grandparents, take the time to think through the situation your child is in. Ask what you can do to give him or her the best help. Offer some suggestions you may have thought about. What does the family need financially?

How can giving be done in the easiest and least painful way? How can your available time be used to their best advantage? Ask specific questions: "Would it help if I came over and watched the children for two hours every other morning?" "Would this be a good weekend for me to take the children?" This is the best way to discover what you can do to help during the difficult time of a divorce.

In chapter 2 we talked about inconveniencing ourselves to meet the needs of our wonder-years grandchildren. We need to be willing to do the same to help our children during a divorce, thereby helping our grandchildren as well.

To do this we may first have to deal with the anger we feel toward our children for putting their kids in this position. Both spouses were probably at fault for the lack of success in the marriage. You may have even "seen it coming" and warned them. They may have made bad choices along the way to the divorce, choices you cautioned them about beforehand. You must remember that they probably already know that. Most people feel horrible about what is happening. They feel like failures, even though they may have done all they could to make it work. They do not need Mom or Dad telling them how wrong, stupid, or immature they are. And even if they are, all we will accomplish by telling them is to alienate them when they need us the most. Deal with your anger yourself. Don't fill your children's lives with "I told you so." Be available to them as a resource in this time of crisis. See it as an opportunity to minister to your child and grandchildren. They don't need your disgust; they need your love and support.

You might want to encourage your child to seek the help of a reputable Christian marriage counselor. Couples experiencing severe marital problems need someone to help them work objectively through their relationship difficulties. You may have to urge your child to consider counseling, but it just may save the marriage. Even if the couple divorces, your child might still benefit greatly from a Christian counselor's assistance.

Patty stayed with Pam and Mike for six months. During that time, Pam and Mike purchased all the food, occasionally babysat, and included Patty and Jason in their lives. After six months, Patty had saved enough money to get an apartment of her own. When they were asked if they regretted anything, Pam and Mike agreed on this: "We are sorry the divorce happened. We still hope and pray for reconciliation, though it doesn't seem likely. But we loved being with our daughter again. And we were delighted to be with Jason during those crucial months of his life and to get to know him better. We are better parents and grandparents because of this experience."

*Establish clear boundaries around your role as a grandparent.* Mike and Pam struggled with what their role should be during this critical time. Sometimes they felt that they were parenting Jason. They neither wanted nor sought this role. Their daughter, who was struggling with her own feelings about herself, sometimes seemed to let them parent both her and her child. This is not what Mike and Pam wanted. They just wanted to help, not go back to parenting, especially parenting their daughter *and* their grandson.

Establishing clear boundaries around your role as grandparent is the third key to effective grandparenting during divorce. As we lend support and encouragement, and as we make our resources available to our children and grandchildren, everyone involved must understand that we are not becoming surrogate parents. Our role is completely different. We are there to lend support and love; we are not there to take over the job of parenting when our children are preoccupied and under great stress. We can assist them, but we must not replace them.

Grandparents must not enable their children to abandon their parental roles by allowing parental responsibility to slide over to themselves. Nor should they take it because they enjoy it. Many grandparents are eager to assume a parental role. But research shows that grandparents who take on the parenting responsibilities lose the sense of satisfaction, adventure, and fun that is so crucial to their well-being as grandparents. One grandparent expressed it this way: "I've already raised my own children. I love my grandchildren, and I want to help my daughter through her divorce. But I'm not the child's parent, and I don't want to act like one. Besides, I don't know what my health will be like in a couple years."

We must draw the line sharply between parenting and grandparenting if we are going to grandparent successfully. The only way to achieve this is to let our children know exactly what we will do and what we think is inappropriate. If we don't communicate this to our children, they won't know where the line is. They may wonder, for example, if it's okay for them to ask us to feed their children or put them to bed. They may wonder if we are beginning to resent these tasks. Grandparents remove the ambiguity when they draw the boundaries realistically and clearly. Do not be afraid of hurting your daughter or son's feelings. The chances of hurt feelings are far more likely when our thinking is not made known, clearly, lovingly, and precisely.

*Maintain contact with both parents.* Grandparents must remember that they have the right and responsibility to maintain contact with their grandchildren following a divorce. This can be especially difficult when custody has been awarded to the parent who is not their child. Grandparents often stop trying to see their grandchild, giving up hope that they can be a presence and influence in their grandchild's life. But it may not have to be this way.

At the most basic level, all states require grandparents to prove that the visits they seek are in the best interest of the grandchild. This generally means grandparents must show that their visits won't be harmful in any way, and that they aren't abusive or otherwise dangerous to the child. Beyond this initial hurdle, each state has a different threshold for when it will allow grandparents to take a case to court.

In June of 2000, the United States Supreme Court issued a decision on grandparents' visitation rights in the Troxel v. Granville case. They canceled out a Washington State law that permitted judges to grant visitation to *any* interested party so long as the visits were in the best interest of the child—even if the parents objected. This court decision limited grandparents' rights, which had been established in most states.

Grandparents will maintain contact more easily if they establish a good relationship with the custodial parent. Earlier in the chapter, we urged grandparents to avoid taking sides and rushing to judgment. Keeping in contact with your grandchildren and both parents after the divorce is one reason for doing this. It is better for the children (and their parents) if you avoid establishing an antagonistic relationship. Otherwise the children once again are forced to handle severely divided loyalties. Do your best not to put them in that position.

Mothers are still awarded custody in a majority of cases in the United States. If you are the paternal grandparent, do your best to maintain a loving relationship with the children's mother. Remember, blame usually can be assigned to both parents. By refusing to lay all the blame on your daughter-in-law, you improve the possibility of having a good relationship with her, which will open the door to maintaining contact with your precious grandchildren.

Grandparents can be given legal rights (in some cases) to spend time with their grandchildren. More important, however, is their moral responsibility to maintain contact following a divorce—especially if they want to be an ongoing influence in the lives of their grandchildren.

Children whose grandparents have stayed in contact with them and have played an important role in their development are much less likely to have struggles and difficulties later. Research shows that it is usually in the best interest of the child to have continuing contact with the grandparents. The reason is clear: Involved grandparents help their grandchildren cope with the trauma of divorce and growing up afterward. Therefore, grandparents have a moral responsibility to help their grandchildren "grow up divorced." Children need the stability and strength and love their grandparents can give them. Your grandchildren desperately need you, whether they recognize it or not. Don't let them down by failing to do your best to maintain contact, difficult though it may be.

When a family experiences a divorce, everyone suffers. It can be especially difficult for the children. They often feel alone and insecure. They are at the mercy of frightening forces they do not understand and cannot change. By not rushing to judgment, by making ourselves and our resources available, by drawing clear boundaries, and by maintaining contact, we can offer these children the support they need.

## Grandparenting during a Family Crisis

During a time of family crisis, grandparents carry a special responsibility and burden. We can help our children through a crisis. We can be an invaluable resource to our children and grandchildren during the dark and stressful days.

Crisis often strikes without warning. It leaves no time for preparation. Judy can still remember how her heart sank into her stomach. She cannot forget the knot of nausea she felt as she drove from her office to the accident. Jack's call had been confusing: "Mom, I'm calling from somebody's car phone on I-96. We've been in an accident. Jay and Erin are all right. Can you come? Please hurry!" Looking back, Judy remembers wondering as she drove to the scene what life would be like without one of her grandchildren. How could she deal with that? How could she support the parents in their time of loss if her own heart was broken? She arrived at the scene in time to watch the paramedics strap one-year-old Jay to a stretcher and slide him into an ambulance. His three-year-old sister Erin left next, and then her son Jack. She prayed as she drove to the hospital, "Oh, God, please take care of them. Don't let them be hurt badly. Please, God, let them be all right. Please!"

The scene at the hospital was both alarming and reassuring. Erin and Jay were bruised and frightened, but news soon came that they were okay. Seatbelts had saved them from serious injury.

But Jack, who was driving when his car struck another car at seventy miles per hour, was not doing well. Chest X-rays showed a problem with his heart. The doctors spoke of "deceleration" and the need for "an immediate heart catheterization." Judy's joy at hearing the children were fine was swept aside by this troubling news. As she sat in the hospital with family and friends, she felt terrified. What if he died? How do you grandparent children who have lost their father?

The silence was overwhelming. Jack had been gone for a long time. Just as the heaviness seemed unbearable, the doctor briskly walked in. "I think Jack's going to be okay." Everyone breathed easier. "We were afraid his heart had been ruptured and that he was bleeding internally. We don't think that is the case now, but we want to keep him overnight to watch him." The doctor talked on, but Judy was no longer listening. She was deeply thankful that her son's life was spared, and that her grandchildren still had their father.

The loss of a parent or child may render some family members incapable of functioning for a time. Families dealing with death and loss need time to weep, to grieve. Grandparents can be a vital resource during these times of sorrow and adjustment if they will follow three guidelines.

*Be there.* The very presence of a loving grandparent is reassuring to a child who has to deal with the fact that Daddy is not going to come home from the hospital. The sense of well-being that comes from Grandma and Grandpa's steady presence cannot be overestimated. When some teenagers were asked what they most wanted from their grandparents during a crisis, they replied, "Being there." Why? Because it signified to them that they would get through, that life would stabilize again.

The presence of Grandma and Grandpa is a solid source of comfort and help. We provide warm, accepting, understanding shoulders to cry on. We can help with common chores that seem overwhelming under the burden of grief. We can drive the children to school. We can make lunch or take care of dinner. We can gently help with the funeral arrangements, lending wisdom and experience gained over the years. Most of all, we can provide a sense of faith, security, and connectedness.

*Be a source of faith.* When families are running short of trust in God, grandparents can express and model their faith in God. It's difficult to feel that a loving God is in control when you've watched your little girl die slowly in a hospital after only three weeks of life. It's unbelievably tough for children to understand how God could let their mom or dad or sibling die. It usually isn't much help when a well-meaning friend quotes Scripture and talks about God's providence, although these things are certainly true. The tragedy is easier to accept when Grandma tearfully tells you that her third child died of polio. As she expresses the pain that was part of that loss, telling you how the presence and power of God carried her through, she brings you comfort and hope. And it's reassuring to see Grandpa on his knees every morning and overhear him speak to God on behalf of his family.

Faith in God is vital and reassuring during a tragedy. Those who have it see their way through the struggles; those who don't have more difficulty moving on with their lives. As grandparents, our living, vital relationship with Jesus can be an inspiration to the whole family. The apostle Paul writes,

> Blessed be the God and Father of our Lord Jesus Christ,
> the Father of mercies and God of all comfort, who

comforts us in all our tribulation, that we may be able to comfort those who are in any trouble, with the comfort with which we ourselves are comforted by God. For as the sufferings of Christ abound in us, so our consolation also abounds through Christ. (2 Corinthians 1:3–5)

On the basis of these verses, most grandparents have earned the right to speak of God's comfort during a tragedy. Their faith has carried them through many rough places and difficult times. They have been taught by the years, not only by sermons and books. Grandparents who have learned the hard-taught lessons of faith must share what they have learned with their grieving, questioning families.

*Express your own grief.* If your grandchild is being buried, please don't feel that you have to keep up a strong facade "so you don't upset the children." Your grief is real, and you must take your place as a mourner. It's not your job to bear all the family burdens at the expense of your own emotional and spiritual health. Give yourself the freedom to express your grief. Let the loss show. It's important for your children and grandchildren to see your grief. By expressing your sorrow, you let your grandchildren know that it's okay for them to cry too. Feeling a deep sense of sadness and loss following the death of a loved one is natural; it is not a sign of weak faith. Let your grandchildren see you grieve, but not as those "who have no hope" (1 Thessalonians 4:13).

I remember when my own dad died several years ago at the age of ninety. At the funeral, my then seventeen-year-old granddaughter Erin slipped out of line with her parents and into the row in which I was sitting. She sat next to me with her arm around me during the service. Afterward, I asked her why she didn't sit with her parents. She said, "I thought it was the right thing to do." She sensed that I needed her comfort more than her parents. She was there to help me as I grieved for the loss of my dad. It meant a lot for me then and the memory of that day is still fresh with me, many years later.

About one year later Erin, Judy, and I were on a plane coming back from a ski trip in Utah. As the plane landed and we were able to use our cell phones, I received a call from a family member telling me that my mother had just died. Once again Erin was at my side to put her arm around her grieving grandfather. She learned from her grandfather that it is not only okay to grieve, but necessary. Someday she too will experience loss, and she will be more prepared to grieve and mourn during that difficult time.

In times of loss, creative grandparents need to feel free to talk about loss, grieve freely, and help their children and grandchildren grieve and mourn. Grandparents need to be *with* their grandchildren in these difficult times, and they need to be especially sensitive. They don't need to use many words; their presence is enough.

Judy and I have admired grandparents who have come through family divorce and death with flying colors. Some of them have done all the right things, but most of all, they have been present for their children and grandchildren. As a counselor, I have seen grandparents become the glue that held the family together during a severe crisis such as a serious accident, death, or divorce.

Creative grandparents are willing to deal with life head-on. We accept its twists and turns, its wide-open pathways and sudden dead ends. We know and accept that life is difficult. We have learned that being alive means bearing pain.

But we also know that life's greatest joys come through its deepest trials. And we remember the promises of the One who said that "He would never leave us or forsake us," the One who referred to himself as the "God of all comfort," and the One who commanded us to "bear one another's burdens" with sensitivity, love, and grace.

# CHAPTER 8

# Across Miles, Mountains, and Oceans

The birth of Jim and Dianne's first child brought grand-parents Ken and Joyce great joy. Ken and Joyce were deeply involved in Katie's life right from the beginning, and they planned to be her lifelong friends. They eagerly antici-pated experiencing the world again through her beautiful blue eyes, and it was happening. Joyce especially took to this little girl, and she felt her love was returned tenfold by Katie. Life was just about perfect for Ken and Joyce. Katie lived only thirty minutes away, and they saw her often. They felt sure, as we often do when life is going our way, that everything would continue to stay the same.

Ken was a successful and beloved pastor. He had urged his congregation many times to give their children to God. He had even pounded the pulpit for emphasis as he said,

"Don't hold back your children from the Lord's service. Our prayer should be that our children will grow up wanting to serve God." He and Joyce sincerely believed what he was saying. It was easy to tell others to be selfless and sacrificial.

Shortly after Katie's second birthday, they learned that Jim, Dianne, and Katie were moving. This was not to be an ordinary move; they were leaving the United States to be missionaries in South America.

Ken and Joyce watched sadly as their daughter, son-in-law, and granddaughter boarded the plane that would take them first to Miami, and then to Montevideo, Uruguay. They faced a future that did not have Katie nearby to light up their lives with her smile and loving hugs. As they drove home, the questions began to come. How were they going continue to be a part of Katie's life? Since she was only two, would she recognize them when she returned after the four years Jim and Dianne were committed to serve? How could they be a positive influence on her life when she was thousands of miles away?

Grandparenting from a distance is increasingly common in today's world. Although most will not have to deal with the distance or duration Ken and Joyce did, many grandparents are forced to cope with the reality of considerable miles between them and the grandchildren they love.

Sometimes grandparents retire and move to warmer southern and western climes to enjoy life in their later years. They are also choosing to say good-bye to their grandchildren. Divorce may mean relocation for the custodial parent, sometimes far from Grandma and Grandpa. The increasing mobility of our culture contributes to the rise of long-distance grandparenting. Parents change jobs, are transferred, or relocate more now than ever. Gone are the days of growing up, attending school, and working all your life in the same town your father did. These factors all contribute to the growing number of grandparents who must find ways to fulfill their important role from a distance.

Grandparenting is a time-intensive activity. The prerequisite to being involved in the lives of your grandchildren is being there. If we do not see them regularly, we feel that we cannot be a major part of their lives. And distance often determines how frequently we see them. Andrew Cherlin in *The New American Grandparent* tells us that grandparents who live within ten miles of their grandchildren average forty visits per year with them, while those who live more than one hundred miles away average only three visits per year. Distance is the single most important factor influencing the amount of time grandparents spend with their grandchildren. Long-distance grandparents are at a severe disadvantage, and so are their grandchildren.

If you live far from your grandchildren, you may be asking the same questions Ken and Joyce were. How can we be a factor in the lives of our grandchildren when so many miles separate us?

In this chapter we will look first, and without flinching, at the pain of grandparenting from a distance. Then we will analyze the problems associated with long-distance grandparenting. We will examine the possibilities for long-distance grandparents who want to be involved in the lives of their faraway grandchildren. Fortunately, technology has made it possible to stay connected across oceans and miles. Finally, we will talk about the preparation required to make visits with them enjoyable and productive.

## The Pain of Long-Distance Grandparenting

As Joyce talked about Katie, her eyes filled with tears and her voice was hoarse with emotion. Saying good-bye had been painful and difficult. She had enjoyed being an involved grandmother with Katie, and they had bonded deeply. It hurt to see her leave. Yet every long-distance grandmother goes for lengthy periods of time without seeing her grandchildren. Every one of those grandparents hurts with each separation. We must face it. Pain is part of long-distance grandparenting.

Grandparents who see their little loved ones infrequently speak of missing the little things that make up their personalities.

"I miss the way he says his *s*'s when he says, 'Pleathe puth me in the thwing again, Grandpa.'

"I miss having her crawl into bed with me during a thunderstorm. She doesn't make a big deal of it. She just slips quietly down the hall and into Grandma's room. Then she reaches over for my hand, squeezes it, and goes back to sleep."

"I miss him bringing his girlfriends over to my house so I can get to meet them. He always tells me, 'I don't want to date someone you don't like, Grandma.'"

"I miss the big hugs and kisses."

"I miss roasting hot dogs in the fireplace, and messy marshmallows burned to a crisp."

"I missed seeing him take his first steps and ride his bike the first time without training wheels. I wish I could have been there for that."

Each of these grandparents is expressing the same sentiment. They miss being with their grandchildren, seeing them grow and thrive, and it brings them pain. They get notes like this:

*Dear Grandma,*

*Thank you for the birthday present. I miss you. I wish you were here. Will you come and visit us soon? It's snowing a lot here, is it snowing in Iowa? I got nice presents for my birthday.*

*Love, Molly*

Pain is part of long-distance grandparenting. But pain is just one of the problems. Grandparents with many miles between them and their grandchildren must also find answers to these difficult questions:

- How can I be a positive influence?
- How can I get to know my grandchildren when I seldom see them?
- Will they get to know me? Will they remember me?
- What can I expect from my grandchildren when I do see them?

These are questions without easy answers. The truth is that it is more difficult to grandparent from a distance than when the children are close. But it is not impossible. You can be a creative, involved grandparent, even though half a continent or half the world separates you from those grandchildren you love. It takes careful thought, lots of planning, some creativity, and a willingness to accept the challenge. But you can do it. So get your creative juices flowing and observe how some other grandparents are succeeding at being long-distance grandparents.

## Creative Ways to Grandparent from a Distance

Ken and Joyce made a playroom in their house that was Katie's exclusive domain. They haven't changed it since she left. They wonder how their two-year-old granddaughter will be able to remember her favorite places at Grandma's house when she probably won't be there again until she is six years old. Their solution is to use modern technology to make a video of the places Katie enjoyed. On the video is the swing set in the park, the room she slept in when she visited Grandma and Grandpa, and her own playroom—complete with play stove, table and chairs, and tea set. As Katie grows older, it will serve as a visual reminder that even though they are far away, her grandparents still love her and are thinking about her.

Video cameras seem to have been invented for long-distance grandparents. Try to get your hands on one for at least a couple days every year. Most digital photography cameras have recording capability, as do many cell phones. They are all invaluable tools for keeping in touch with your grandchildren.

One grandparent wanted to teach his Christian values to his teenage grandson. So he borrowed a video camera and narrated the tale of his youthful adventures. He had footage of the exact places his mistakes were made. He filmed the sharp curve in the road where he had crashed his car when driving while drinking. He told his grandson how he had nearly died.

He went to the junk yard to see if the first car he ever owned was still there, because in that car he had stolen his first kiss. As he told the story, he gave some clear warnings about relating with girls. He narrated many of the experiences of his life in the video, passing along the lessons he learned and the values he had grown to accept.

When the package with the DVD arrived, his grandson was at first disappointed. No money was in the package. He let the video sit unwatched for several days. Then one evening his parents returned home to find him sprawled in front of the TV, watching as Grandpa narrated his life story. This apparently nonchalant teen was enthralled by the tales of his grandfather's youth. Grandpa had succeeded in teaching his grandson about life and his faith in God through the use of technology.

Through video, grandparents can also help grandchildren visualize what an upcoming visit with Grandma and Grandpa will be like. Grandparents can record some of the fun places they might go and things they might do. There could be scenes from the mall, zoo, beach, backyard, or park. Viewing the video would excite the children about visiting Grandma and Grandpa.

The uses creative grandparents could make of a video camera are limited only by their imagination—and their patience with learning how to run the camera.

The telephone is another way for creative grandparents to be a positive influence on their faraway grandchildren, especially when used with a little imagination. If Grandpa and grandson share a common love for baseball, for example, they could watch the World Series together and text each other after a great play or hit that puts their team ahead. Sure, it costs money—but it's cheaper than a plane ticket! It's simple to get out your cell phone, write a short text, and send it to your waiting grandson. Text your grandson after key plays to applaud or criticize the players or berate the umpires for their obviously impaired vision. The same could be done in watching your favorite TV shows together, or for special programs in which you and your granddaughter are both interested.

The telephone can also be a way to spend regularly scheduled time with your granddaughter or grandson. Grandmother, for example, can have a regularly scheduled Saturday morning or Sunday afternoon phone date with her grand-daughter. It's a time when they share news from the past week, and they can enjoy the sound of each other's voice. All it takes is the desire to make it a priority and the approval of Mom and Dad.

Hip grandparents can also send messages to their grand-child on Facebook or by e-mail. They can send pictures, videos, and drawings, and share links to articles and videos about common interests. Imagine the surprise of a teenager who receives an e-mail from Grandma telling about her trip to the Grand Canyon—complete with pictures of her astride a horse on the South Rim. Once again, a little desire and imagination makes excellent communication possible.

Some truly high-tech grandparents connect with their teenage grandchildren through programs like Skype, which allow real-time video and phone chatting at a low cost. One grandfather, after telling me about the importance of regular contact with his grandchildren, mentioned that he was mov-ing to Florida for the next six months. I was about to ask how he could leave the grandchildren he adored when he said, "We will talk to them nearly every day we are gone. They Skype me so I get to see their faces and talk to them almost daily." Most computers come equipped with a webcam, but if your computer doesn't have one, the tiny camera can be installed at a reasonable cost. Ask your grandchildren how Skype works. They will help you set up the program.

If you are not into technology, how about writing every week? As often as possible, enclose a photo of you doing something lively and interesting. The letter does not have to be as literary as Hemingway reporting on the running of the bulls. "Hi! How are you doing? I think about you a lot and

I wondered how you were getting along. This is me playing golf." This kind of note will do the job.

Letter writing is a great way from some of us who have difficulty verbalizing our feelings to tell our grandchildren what they mean to us. What we may not be able to say to their faces, we can put into words on paper and send off. All grandchildren, no matter what age, like to hear that Grandma or Grandpa thinks they're great.

To make it even more special, you might want to purchase matching stationery for you and each grandchild. Explain to them that this stationery is to be used only when you write one another. Imagine the excitement when the special envelope comes! It means a letter from Grandma! Specialness always makes children (and grandparents) feel loved and unique.

The mail is also a way to share common interests, or to exchange information about important events. The grandson who sends Grandma a picture of his little sister as well as a running commentary on his latest Little League exploits will warm her heart. Likewise, grandparents can send baseball cards to their collecting grandson or granddaughter. Or they can send press clippings or magazine articles about their grandchild's favorite athletes, television stars, or music personalities.

A brave grandfather may listen to the music his grandchildren like. He could even send them tickets to a concert in their area. He passes along his grousing about the lyrics and beat, of course. But they love Grandpa's reviews of the latest from the Jonas Brothers or Taylor Swift.

Once again, the limit to your involvement with grandchildren who live far away is determined more by the intensity of your desire to be their friend and a creative, involved grandparent than it is by the miles that separate you. Some grandparents who live on the same block as their grandchildren are not involved in their lives. It's a matter of choice and priority. The question is this: How much do we want to make a difference in the lives of our distant grandchildren? Do we care enough to watch a game with them and text them on the cell phone? Do we want to stay in touch enough to write regularly? Will we go to the trouble and expense to purchase or rent a video camera? I hope so!

We can be a positive influence on our grandchildren from miles away. It takes energy and ingenuity, but we can do it!

## Getting to Know You

Using the methods introduced above, we can get to know our long-distance grandchildren and let them get to know us. If you choose letter writing, you might try the following:

- Initiate a writing project. Challenge the grandchildren to write about their activities, friends, school, and feelings.
- Provide the grandchildren with a written history of the family. Use one of those books with blank pages and lines, and fill it in with important dates, events, descriptions, and memories. Include pictures and sketches.
- Write about interesting events from your childhood, teenage years, college days, or military experience. Pass along your good childhood memories. Tell the funny stuff.
- Write about some of the hard times: long months without a job, empty cupboards during the Depression, Grandma's slow recovery from an illness. Describe

what happened when your brother broke his leg. Create a sense of family strength and courage.

- Have the grandchildren describe a typical school day or tell you what they do on Sunday.
- Ask the younger children to draw a picture of something they enjoyed doing or somewhere they went.
- Describe for the grandchildren a fun experience or trip you enjoyed. Be sure to talk about feelings, insights, and reflections.
- Include a lot of humor. Show them that life can be fun even when it's serious and difficult.

These are ways of letting your grandchildren into your life by letter, and of getting into theirs. You'll soon discover you don't feel like strangers when you are able to get together. You'll already have plenty to talk about.

Never overlook your camera as a means of enhancing your relationship with your faraway grandchildren. You will communicate volumes about yourself and your life through pictures. Grandmother Nancy, who lives in New Jersey, regularly sends photographs as postcards to her Michigan grandchildren. She draws a line down the middle of the back of the picture, puts the name, address, and stamp on the proper side, jots a short note explaining the photo, and drops it in the mail. This helps her grandchildren keep her face fresh in their minds. They know what her interests are, and they have a pretty clear idea of what her home and her part of the country is like. And these "picture postcards" always end up on the refrigerator door or on the bulletin boards in the children's rooms. One of our adult grandchildren who lives out of town keeps what we send her on her bulletin board at work. These mementos keep us connected no matter the physical distance between us.

Your grandchildren need to know that you do more than sit in a rocking chair and knit sweaters. Explain through letters, photos, and videos what your life is all about. Let your grandchildren get a feel for your eccentric friends—and your own humorous quirks as well. Yes, you can let them deep into your life even though you are not nearby.

A great-grandmother lived in Montana. Because of poor health and economic factors, she never got to see her faraway grandchildren. But they knew her as Momma Montana. They heard from her frequently, and they knew that she loved them. Her picture went up on the bulletin boards in their rooms, along with other family photos. They prayed for her, along with the rest of the family.

It would be simple to sit in our easy chairs and complain about the miles that keep us from getting to know our grandchildren. How much better to get up out of that chair and do something about it!

Arthur Kornhaber, a researcher and grandparent himself, wrote, "Too many grandparents, when they retire, are dropping out of family life and abandoning their grandchildren. Instead of running off to the Sun Belt to play shuffleboard in the sun, their goal as grandparents should be to nurture the younger generations, and to play an active role as emotional leaders of the extended family." This can be done from a distance, if we are willing to stretch our imaginations and drop some of our inhibitions.

## When They Visit You

A final ingredient of long-range grandparenting is preparation for visits. To make the most of the short time long-distance grandparents and their grandchildren have together, be sure to prepare for visits in advance. This is important whether we go to see our grandchildren or they come to visit us.

It's a treat to have our grandchildren all to ourselves. There is something special about being their only companions for a few days or a week or more. We enjoy seeing them outside their usual environment and having them in our world. Often, however, the anticipation is more fun than the actual visit because we have not prepared properly. We feel relieved when they leave, yet we also feel guilty because we didn't do all we could have with them. Careful forethought and simple planning can go a long way toward ensuring that the next visit is more satisfying.

We must first answer some basic questions. Are our grandchildren old enough to travel "all by themselves" for a visit? How often should they come? Should we offer to pay all the expenses, including travel? What will we do with them while they are here?

In his book *How to Grandparent*, Fitzhugh Dodson recommends that children should be at least five years old before they visit on their own. Most airlines permit children of this age to travel alone on an airplane. You may fret at the idea of a five-year-old traveling solo, but the airlines do a wonderful job of taking care of their little passengers. They assist them with boarding and deplaning, and they give them special attention and companionship during a layover or change of planes. As long as you are there on time to meet them, they should not experience any difficulty.

Your young grandchild will almost certainly experience some homesickness on the visit. But that is not crippling and usually can be dealt with by wise parental preparation and understanding grandparents. Bringing along a much-loved doll or stuffed animal may help. So will a reminder of how many days before he or she sees Mom and Dad again. A phone call home may become necessary, but try to save it as a last resort.

Before you suggest a visit to the child, be sure to talk it over with the parents and get their okay. Discuss the logistics of travel and time before extending the invitation to the child. Nothing is more aggravating to a parent than to have to be the bad guy and say no to a child because Grandpa went ahead and scheduled a visit without clearing it with Mom and Dad first.

As for the length of the visit, it is important to know your grandchildren. If you live on a remote island off the coast of Maine and your grandchildren are city dwellers, two weeks could seem like an eternity to you and to them. On the other hand, if you live in Orlando, a visit of two weeks might not be long enough to do everything. Keep this principle in mind: Try to arrange for your grandchildren to leave wishing they could have stayed longer rather than waiting sullenly for the departure date. As a general rule, start with a visit of just a few days. As your grandchildren grow and mature, adjust the length of the visits accordingly.

How often should grandchildren visit? When should they visit? The answer to these questions depends on you and their parents. How much free time do you have? Will you be taking vacation time to be with them? Are you retired? How much energy do you have? Do you have the means to fly your grandchildren to your home more than once a year? Or is every other year your limit? Only you can answer these questions. Perhaps the parents could cover the cost of one visit and you the next. Once again, your individual situation will determine the frequency and length of the visits. Even a family of modest means can scrimp and watch for special airfares for a visit to Grandma when it's made a priority.

Summer vacation is usually a great time for most school-age grandchildren to visit Grandma and Grandpa. Around the middle of July, mothers and fathers will appreciate a break from their active, vacationing children. By then the children are growing bored with doing the same old things at home and are often driving Mom and Dad up the wall.

If grandparents live in the Sun Belt and their grandchildren reside in the frozen Midwest or Northeast, Christmas break is a good time for a visit. Do not interfere with the family's Christmas celebration by unexpectedly proposing that the grandchildren spend the holiday with you. Most parents would rather spend Christmas with their family together, and they should. Christmas is a wonderful family tradition.

You might propose flying the children out just after Christmas and have them return after New Year's Day. Remember, always schedule the trip with the parents before discussing it with your grandchildren.

You might talk about two or three possible dates for a visit, including spring break, and letting the children themselves decide, especially if they are older and parents allow them to make some decisions themselves. This gives the grandchildren a feeling of control and ownership over the trip. It will also keep them from feeling that they've been shipped off to get them out of Mom and Dad's hair.

The most important question facing grandparents when their grandchildren visit is this: What will we do with them once they get here? After we have hugged and kissed at the airport, stopped at their favorite restaurant on the way home, and unpacked, what do we do? Here are four principles to follow when planning activities for your visiting grandchildren, whether they are five or fifteen years of age.

*Be available.* The first and most important key to a happy, satisfying visit is to loosen up your schedule to accommodate your grandchildren. I know grandparents who look forward all year to a visit from their grandchildren, but then refuse to cancel a golf match or pass up their regular Thursday brunch with the girls. You need to maximize your availability while the grandchildren are there. If you are not yet retired, take some time off. Find a substitute for the golf or summer bowling league. Grandchildren—especially the younger ones—will be disappointed if they have to play second fiddle to Grandma or Grandpa's packed schedule.

Our bingo games or women's clubs are not nearly as important as our grandchildren. For that matter, neither are business meetings or board meetings. This is your time with your grandchildren. As long-distance grandparents, your time with these precious children is already restricted. When they are able to come, let them know how important they are and how much you love them by rescheduling your lives around them. Even the youngest grandchildren will realize what you have done, and it will communicate your love very clearly.

When you talk to the parents after a visit, never make a big deal about what you had to give up to spend time with your grandchildren. Their response may be, "If it's such a big sacrifice, Dad, forget it. It's easier for us to keep them at home anyway. You don't have to worry about putting yourself out again, because you won't be given the opportunity." Creative grandparents willingly give their time to their grandchildren to watch them grow and find joy in their presence. Be available!

*Be flexible.* Flexibility is a vital factor in making your grandchildren's visit a success. We often look forward so eagerly to these rare opportunities with our grandchildren that we create rigid, unrealistic expectations of what the week will be like. We expect our grandchildren to leap into our arms immediately and love us completely and without reservation. That's not the way it usually works. Younger grandchildren may take a couple of days to warm up to a grandma or grandpa they haven't seen for many weeks or months. Older grandchildren may be embarrassed by your affection, or they may wonder if you will like the changes they have undergone since you last saw them. Don't put enormous pressure on them, or yourself, to keep your relationship the same. Over time we all change. Our grandchildren grow up and become interested in different activities. As we change, our relationships change. Don't view these changes as negative. Just try to be flexible—adapt and make the changes work for you and your grandchild. Don't try to relive past moments of glory every year. And don't expect the week to be one enormous success after another (by your definitions).

One grandmother treasured the yearly visits of her two young grandchildren. She lived on an old farm and they lived in the city. Every year they visited, they worked together in the garden and the children loved it. They would go to the woods and fields behind the house to pick wild strawberries and blueberries. It was a tradition Grandma and grandchildren looked forward to. Grandma would use the fresh fruit they picked in a pie for dessert after dinner. But when the oldest granddaughter, Tara, turned thirteen, she didn't want to pick berries anymore. She was more interested in the boy who lived on the farm down the road. Grandma was hurt and angry. What was wrong with Tara? Why couldn't she just do what she always did? Was she trying to be difficult?

The answer to these questions, of course, is no. Tara was growing up. Her needs and interests had changed as her body had changed. Grandma made the mistake of assuming her thirteen-year-old granddaughter was the same as the seven-year-old who had eaten more wild strawberries than she had put in the bucket. The girl had changed, and Grandma's expectations needed to change and adapt as well.

One sure way to wreck a visit with your grandchildren is to weigh it down with expectations. Be flexible. Realize that a year or even six months can make a tremendous difference in your grandchild. It might be a good idea not to schedule the first few days too full of activities they loved on the previous visit. Use that time to get to know the children again, determine where they are, and discover what they like to do. Find a place that's comfortable for both of you and build on it.

*Establish traditions.* Being flexible does not preclude the establishment of family traditions. Large and small traditions provide continuity for grandparents and grandchildren who see each other infrequently. They can provide a starting point for the renewal of a dormant relationship. When these traditions are not laden with weighty expectations, they can provide a safe and familiar means of remembering and renewing the relationship.

Jerry and I (Judy) lived a considerable distance from my parents when our children were small. Sometimes the infrequency of the visits made our first few hours together somewhat awkward. My son Jon had a solution for this. His grandma always baked yellow cupcakes with vanilla frosting when she knew the boys were coming. When we arrived, Jon never even tried to enter into small talk with his grandparents. He went right to the kitchen of the rambling old farmhouse in search of Grandma's cupcakes. His first words were invariably the same, "Grandma, where are the cupcakes? I've been thinking about them the whole trip." What started as a simple, onetime event became a tradition that eased grandparents and grandchildren into a warm relationship.

The tradition continued fifteen years. On each trip to Grandma's, Jon and Jack would talk about having a cupcake before doing anything else. Grandma loved it. Even after Jon became an adult with children of his own, he continued to go to the kitchen every time he visited his grandmother to find the cupcakes.

This is a simple tradition. Other traditions carry much more significance. Grandma Sue couldn't wait for her granddaughter Lisa to arrive for her visit. You see, Lisa had turned ten, and that was a special age for the girls in Grandma Sue's family. Grandma began teaching the girls to sew when they turned ten. Beginning with her first granddaughter nearly fifteen years earlier, she had decided that she would instruct each granddaughter in this skill that she had learned over her lifetime. What began as a desire to pass on something of lifelong use became a tradition. When each granddaughter reached age ten, she spent a week with Grandma Sue during the summer learning to sew. Younger girls always asked, "Can I do it now?" But Sue knew the virtue in patience and the importance of fairness, so each granddaughter had to wait her turn.

When their tenth birthday came and summer vacation began, the girl would receive a formal invitation from Grandma. "Dear Lisa: I would very much like for you to visit me this summer for one week. You are now ten years old, and it would by my pleasure to begin to teach you how to sew." The letter went on, but those somewhat formal words were music to the ears of each girl.

As Grandma grew older, the girls seemed to get younger. Every year it became more difficult to find things to talk about, but there was always the sewing. Some of the girls became adept with the needle and thread. Others never got the hang of it. It didn't matter to Grandma. She treasured the hours they spent together—hours spent over patterns, looking at her granddaughters' beautiful profiles and the way they cocked their heads when really concentrating.

Grandma was hesitant to talk about music or boys when her granddaughters reached their teenage years, but she could usually start a vigorous conversation with, "I remember when you were ten and the first time you put a piece of cloth through a sewing machine . . ." Her granddaughter's face would soften, and the years that separated them would disappear, along with their differences in values and preoccupations. The tradition was a source of strength in their relationship.

Traditions are extremely important in long-distance grandparenting. They provide a point of contact for grandparents and grandchildren. They become a way to remember Grandpa and Grandma. It is difficult to remember them abstractly, but the memories of fishing trips, or daily walks to the store for a newspaper and a candy bar or ice cream, or the bowling outing the first night at the house are easy to remember. Traditions make the miles wear less on the memory.

To lessen the distance between you and your faraway grandchildren, establish traditions. Beware, however, of forcing them on your grandchildren. They need to be fun for everyone involved. Look carefully at the things you now do with your grandchildren. You probably already have traditions in the making. Point them out to your grandchildren. Let them know that you value those traditions as much as they do, that you respect their involvement in them, and that you want them to continue. If your grandchildren outgrow the traditions, let the traditions die. It may be time to establish new traditions appropriate to their age and stage of life.

Traditions become important sources of shared memories and laughter later on. As our precious little grandchildren turn into adults, the warmth we receive from remembering long-standing traditions cannot be overstated. We'll think about them often and the common ground they established as the years go by.

*Let them lead.* A final principle for long-distance visits with grandchildren is to let the children lead. As advised earlier with wonder-years grandchildren, try to follow the children's agenda. During the visit, follow their interests and desires. You have fifty-one other weeks of the year to "do your own thing." When they arrive, let them tell you what they want to do and how they would like to spend their time. Offer them a variety of choices and listen to their suggestions.

Some grandparents give their visiting grandchildren a choice between going bowling at the Starlight Lanes or the Ideal Hour Alleys. In reality, that is not a choice at all. A real choice would be bowling, miniature golf, going to the beach, or shopping at the mall. Let your grandchildren help you decide, and then do it!

Letting them lead means that we are making them the most important people in our lives while they are with us. We say they are the center of our lives, but we are often quite determined to do what we want during visits. Be aware of that temptation and fight it. Giving children a choice in decisions demonstrates our love for them and reinforces their worth and independence.

## When You Visit Them

It's a little different when you go to your grandchildren's home. A successful visit requires use of tact, discretion, and selflessness. The keys to visiting your grandchildren at their home are simple.

*Realize that you are on their turf.* When we arrive from out of town for the purpose of visiting our children and grandchildren, we must remember that we are guests. Our children have busy lives that do not revolve around us, even though they may be thrilled to see us. They may also see us as an inconvenience at times. The first key to having a successful visit is to realize, in Dorothy's words to Toto, "We're not in Kansas anymore." We are not in our environment. We don't make the rules here. Our children do. Guests do not tell the landlord what to do. Guests are polite and abide by the rules of the household. They don't try to set new rules. Our job is to abide by the bedtime set for the children and respect the parents' feelings about candy and their approach to discipline and everything else. Realize where you are.

*Be willing to share your grandchildren.* True, we're the visitors, the guests. But we still have to share those precious children with school, their friends, their parents, and their own interests and activities.

When they visit us, we are usually the focal point of their interest. They are in a strange city. They don't know anyone. By nature they cling to us and make us the center of their universe. When we visit them, it's different. Their everyday activities and friendships continue. Hopefully your children and grandchildren will understand your desire to spend time together, but all we can do is ask in advance for that to occur. We need to be sensitive to their interests and the forces that are pulling them in many directions. All of this means we need to be ready to share our grandchildren.

*Know when to be quiet.* You may not like the way your children discipline their children. Whether they are too strict or too lenient, chances are their approach to discipline won't be to your liking. Stifle the impulse to comment on everything you find wrong. Don't speak to your children about it as if they were eleven years old again. Know when to be quiet. Your children don't mind you acting like a grandparent; they do mind you acting like their parent or trying to parent the grandchildren. We have not been invited to critique our children's parenting skills or to grade them on their methods of discipline. We are there as loving grandparents.

What can be more dangerous than a grandmother who has always been a combination of Mr. Clean and Scrubbing Bubbles? Dust is her enemy, and dirt is anathema. Her son marries a nice girl who is an average housekeeper. Grandma visits, can't stand it, and decides to set new standards for her daughter-in-law. (She may even be secretly concerned about the health of her grandchildren.) So she starts to make remarks and give unsolicited advice. How do you suppose that daughter-in-law feels? Probably like a failure, or angry because Grandma doesn't think she is good enough for her son or grandchildren.

One family handled criticism this way. The son came to his mother and said directly, "Mom, if you can't accept the way we live, go back home, now. I know you love the grandchildren, and we all love you, but there will be no more visits like this one." Grandma sputtered. She cried. But she realized that the house was basically clean, and she accepted the fact that her son was right. She had violated a rule of visiting grandchildren: Know when to be quiet. Now she keeps her thoughts to herself, and the visits continue.

*Learn to be adaptable.* This principle for trouble-free visits to our grandchildren goes beyond being flexible. To be adaptable means not only putting aside your daily rituals and plans, but accepting the rituals and schedule of the household you are visiting. Make the effort to fit in. Your ability to adapt to their routine and lifestyle will make the visit far less stressful and far more pleasant for everyone. It will also guarantee an invitation to return.

Long-distance grandparenting can be a painful, problem-filled experience. Or, with a little planning and creativity, it can be trouble-free and relatively satisfying. It's up to us as creative grandparents. We can let the miles defeat us and turn us into spectators as our grandchildren grow into young men and women, or we can put ourselves into the starting lineup and play a role in their development. Make the effort to be involved. The miles are a hindrance, requiring creativity and ingenuity on your part to connect with your grandchildren. But the miles don't need to stop you from being an important part of your grandchildren's lives.

## CHAPTER 9

# The Beauty of Differences

But you don't understand. My situation is different. We're not the typical mom, dad, and 1.5 children suburban family. I grew up in a small-town Baptist church and married a local boy. But my twice-divorced son just married a Jewish girl from the Bronx, and she has two children from a previous marriage. How is an Indiana farm woman going to grandparent them? And now my son and his new wife are going to have a baby of their own."

The concerned grandmother went on. "Grandparenting for me is not like it was for my mother and grandmother. I can't assume, as they did, that my grandchildren are growing up with my values. Nor can I assume that I will be able to spend a lot of time with them. As a matter of fact, I don't have the slightest clue about how to relate to my new daughter-in-law. My instant grandchildren are six and ten, and they have grown up in New York City. When they came to visit last week, it was the first time in their lives that either of them had seen a real live cow or been to Sunday school. Grandparenting is so different today and seems to be more difficult."

This grandmother has to face issues her grandparents would never have dreamed possible. Grandparents today must be ready to deal creatively with diverse religious backgrounds, cultural dissimilarities, and a plethora of family differences. Most of us prepare for grandparenting with the assumption that our children will grow up, get married, have children, and live happily ever-after. The reality for many families is that "happily ever-after" never happens, or happens quite differently than we had pictured.

In this chapter we will explain how to be creatively involved in your grandchildren's lives when families are different, when values are different, and when children are different. Here are some examples we've come across in our years of working with families.

- Jo is a fifty-eight-year-old African-American grandmother whose pregnant daughter is having a child with a white man. Jo wonders if her daughter is prepared to handle the ethnic and cultural differences in this relationship.

- Bill's daughter has been married three times. She has four children by those marriages. She has just announced that she is moving in with her new boyfriend. Bill is worried about his grandchildren's values, and he wonders if his daughter understands the potential damage she is doing.

- Ken, a grandfather of four, has just announced to his children that he is divorcing their mother. He wonders how this will affect his relationship with his grand-children.

- Amanda is a grandmother of six. She was the first woman in her family to become a medical doctor. Most of her goals for her children, and now her grandchildren, center on their education. Amanda's daughter, who has an MBA, recently married a man without a high school diploma. This is a second marriage for both of them. Amanda is afraid that his lack of education will have a negative influence on her educational goals for her grandchildren.

- Five years ago, Jim's son married a lovely girl who was not a Christian. Last week they brought Jim's first grandchild home from the hospital. Jim is worried that his son and daughter-in-law will not bring up his grandson to love Jesus.

- Reggie is five now, but you wouldn't be able to tell that by talking to him. Reggie is a special-needs child, developmentally disabled. Reggie's grandparents worry about how they will relate to a grandchild with whom they cannot communicate.

- Roger's grandson needs speech therapy. Mark, who is four years old, speaks only a few unclear words. The experts say that his frequent ear infections have contributed to slow speech development. Roger is concerned that his grandson isn't very smart. He's uncomfortable taking Mark out with him because he often has trouble knowing what Mark wants and what he is saying.

Each of the above situations calls for grandparenting with a difference. Ethnic and religious differences, blended families, and special-needs grandchildren present unique challenges to involved, creative grandparents. Many men and women have met those special kinds of challenges without fear. As a result, they have had confident, joyful, and rewarding grandparenting experiences. If you were to talk with these creative grandparents, as we have, they would tell you to follow six principles to enable you to grandparent with a difference.

## 1. Learn to live with your children's choices.

Jo, our first grandmother, carries a great deal of anger toward her daughter. Although she prides herself on her lack of prejudice and her openness, she also prides herself on her family's heritage and ethnic background. She resents the fact that her daughter has put her in an awkward position. She hadn't expected to become a grandmother yet, and she hadn't thought about grandparenting a racially mixed child. She is angry at her daughter and soon-to-be son-in-law, and she is angry at herself for being upset with them. Jo has to learn the first principle of grandparenting with a difference. She needs to learn to live with her children's choices.

We all spend time and energy worrying about things we can't change. Sure, Jo's life would be easier if her daughter had waited until she was married to have a child. Things might have been simpler if she had married an African-American man. But she didn't. And besides, those were not Jo's decisions to make. Her daughter has made her choices, and now it is up to Jo to find a way to live with them.

Wishing that past events had never occurred is futile. We can't turn back the clock and undo the choices our children have made. Our role in the lives of our grandchildren may depend on how well we learn to live with those choices. If our children have to listen to us complain about their decisions every time they see us, they will probably not want to see us very often. That means we will not see our grandchildren very often.

We may hold ourselves responsible for the choices our grown children have made. When they choose well, we applaud our parenting and their good judgment. When we feel they have chosen poorly, we question our parenting and our children's good sense. These reactions are destructive and unnecessary. Grown children must make their own decisions and take responsibility for them. We are responsible only to learn to live with their choices, getting on with the business of loving our child, his or her mate, and our grandchildren.

## 2. Do not punish your grandchildren for your children's choices.

The second principle for grandparenting with a difference is also vitally important. Understand and follow this concept, and grandparenting with a difference will be much easier. We must not punish our grandchildren for our children's choices.

One grandfather has never seen his nine-year-old grandson, even though they live only ten miles apart. His daughter married a man of Asian descent. His negative feelings about Asians date from the Vietnam War, and he has never dealt with them. When his daughter announced her engagement, he threw her out of the house and hasn't spoken to her since. His anger at his daughter's choice is punishing his only grandchild, and punishing himself too. Prejudice has destroyed his opportunity to enjoy his grandson. His grandson is growing up without the presence of his grandparents and the knowledge that his grandfather does not accept him for who he fundamentally is.

We may be angry or disappointed by a decision our son or daughter makes. But we must never turn that anger on our grandchildren. They have done nothing wrong. I am often disappointed by the lack of forgiveness and understanding exercised by some Christians. The grandparent mentioned above is an elder in his church, yet he is not only sinning with his prejudice, but also with his anger. He is sinning, too, in his lack of love toward his daughter, her husband, and especially his grandson. The Bible is clear in its call for love:

> If anyone says, "I love God," yet hates his brother, he is a liar. For anyone who does not love his brother, whom he has seen, cannot love God, whom he has not seen. And he has given us this command: Whoever loves God must also love his brother. (1 John 4:20–21 NIV)

Although John is talking here about loving our brothers in Christ, we can assume that we should also love our own family members.

Disappointment and anger erect huge barriers that we will not or cannot hurdle. You may find yourself reading this book as a surprised and bewildered grandparent. Your unmarried daughter has just given you a grandchild, and you are filled with conflicting feelings of love and anger and joy and disappointment and shame. Don't take those feelings out on your new grandchild. More than anything in the world, your job is to love that little boy. If he's partly of a different race, so be it. If his father is Catholic, Baptist, Jewish, or

Buddhist, love him. Don't punish the child for choices that his parents have made of which you don't understand or approve.

You don't have to turn it into a tragedy when your daughter or son marries somebody from outside your religious background or chooses a mate of a different ethnicity. You don't need to go into high drama when your unmarried son or daughter announces impending parenthood. A greater tragedy occurs when you react with such rage and bitterness that you can never grow close to your grandkids. Biracial babies, babies with same-sex parents, and babies born out of wedlock giggle and laugh just like all babies. They all need to be hugged and loved. New parents of every kind need to know that their parents are behind them with love and support.

### 3. Accept your grandchildren the way they are.

Researchers Marc Baranowski and Gary Schilmoeller remind us of the challenge of grandparents who have a grandchild with a disability: "Grandparents appear to be regarded by many in the helping professions as 'outside' family members, but they are not outside the confusion, sadness, anger, challenge, and joy brought about by the birth and growth of a grandchild who has a disability."

Baranowski and Schilmoeller in their article "Grandparents in the Lives of Grandchildren with Disabilities: Mothers' Perceptions" found that mothers of children with disabilities reported that grandparents assisted most by accepting the grandchild's special needs, spending time with the grandchild, helping care for the grandchild, focusing on the positive qualities of the grandchild, and treating the grandchild as well as other grandchildren. One could summarize their findings by saying that these helpful grandparents accept their grandchildren the way they are.

Remember Reggie's grandparents? Reggie is a special-needs grandchild. His developmental disability has left his grandfather and grandmother concerned about the roles they play in his life. As they watch other grandparents at the zoo talk and laugh with their grandchildren, they know that they will probably never have those opportunities with Reggie. He is wheelchair-bound and unable to communicate verbally. Even so, Reggie's grandparents haven't given up. They have learned the third principle of grandparenting with a difference.

It is futile for Reggie's grandparents to wish that his body would cooperate with his mind. Unless there's a miracle, it's just not going to happen. Instead of stewing in their sorrow, Reggie's grandparents have chosen to accept him as he is, and love him without reservation. They do everything with Reggie they would do with a "normal" grandchild. They take him to the zoo, McDonalds, and the park. In fact, they do more than most grandparents. Realizing his special needs, they help his parents with his therapy and accompany him on his frequent trips to the hospital. Sometimes it's hard for them to see him in his wheelchair. They know the loving little boy trapped inside that damaged body and they wish for his sake that he could run and jump like other little boys. But they have learned that, if Reggie's health is a special heartache, his soul is a special joy. They cannot imagine now what life would be like without him. He has taught them to view life differently. They see every day with Reggie as a gift to be treasured, and they are determined to savor their time with him. They are involved, creative grandparents, and they love their special-needs grandson very much.

The principle of accepting your grandchildren as they are holds true no matter what the special need or difference. If your grandchildren don't go to your church, accept them anyway. If they are not growing up with your values, accept them anyway. If they can't hear or see or walk, love and accept them anyway. This can be difficult. It's one thing to say, and another, much more difficult, thing to do. However, once you make that decision to accept them the way they are and begin to practice it, you will find that it is really not that difficult. Talk to and watch other grandparents who are living with a difference. Learn from them. You will see loving grandparents who live as if there is no difference. They have seen the beauty of differences.

The keys to accepting different grandchildren are honesty and knowledge. Honesty—constant, relentless honesty with ourselves—about how we really feel is vital. We must be honest about our underlying motives, and about our own prejudices and pride. Are we too concerned about what others may think? Are we ashamed of our grandchild? Are we afraid of what our Christian friends at church may say? We must also be honest about the reality of a special need and the prognosis for recovery. Some special-needs grandchildren will surprise us with unexpected growth and maturity, but others may disappoint us with their limitations and lack of growth.

Acceptance is made easier by knowledge. If you are the grandparent of a special-needs grandchild, take the time and effort to understand those needs. Find out about actual abilities, potential, and limitations. Disabled children are often capable of far more than we give them credit. One mother of a special-needs child had to tell her parents repeatedly to stop babying their granddaughter. Although she is sixteen years old, the grandparents, because of her disability, talked to her as if she were five years old. This was degrading for her, and it angered her mother. Observe the child's limitations and possibilities. Work with the limitations and strive for the possibilities. This will enable you to understand your grandchildren better and to accept them more easily.

The same principle holds true when grandparenting children who are being raised in a different religious atmosphere. Again, learn as much as you can. It will provide you with an opportunity to talk to your grandchildren about their religious values. You may find that the differences are not as great as you had feared. One of the easiest ways to build acceptance is to know your grandchildren intimately.

### 4. Work for compromise.

If religious faith is important to us and not to our children, how can we deal with that difference and still help our grandchildren in their development of faith? How do we pass on our moral values to our grandchildren when our children do not share those values? The answer to both of those questions is found in the fourth principle for grandparenting with a difference: Work for compromise.

The words *compromise*, *faith*, and *values* don't usually go together. And we are not suggesting for one minute that grandparents compromise on issues of faith or morality. But let's be realistic. Some opportunity to pass on our faith and moral values is better than none. To have even some chance, we are going to have to stop thinking in terms of winner-take-all. We have to think in terms of the best we can do for our grandchildren.

Issues of faith and morality often present themselves in sharp contrasts. Either you are a Christian or you aren't. Either you believe premarital sex is wrong or you don't. These issues are clearly marked. We think that if we don't chide our children for not attending church or for their lax morals we are implicitly giving their actions our stamp of approval. But wait a minute. This book is not advocating that we abandon our goals of strong moral values for our grandchildren. Nor is it sliding into moral relativism. We believe strongly that some values are *not* open to compromise. These issues are black and white; however, the means of teaching these values to our grandchildren are not so clear.

Maryanne is a devout Christian. Her daughter hasn't been to church in years. Maryanne feels strongly that her grandchildren should be in church at least once a week. Her daughter doesn't care, and she usually sleeps in on Sunday. Maryanne has repeatedly asked her daughter if she could take her grandchildren to church with her. Because her daughter doesn't like getting up and getting them dressed for church, she always says no. At this point Maryanne has a choice. She could become angry, storm out of the house, and go to church for the rest of her life without her grandchildren. But Maryanne knows the value of compromise. She rightly figured that some church is better than no church at all. So she suggested to her daughter that twice a month her grandchildren could stay with her on Saturday night, and she would take them to church with her on Sunday. Her daughter agreed! Maryanne loves being with her grandchildren every other weekend, and is able to attend church with them. She did not compromise her goal of developing her grandchildren's faith, but by compromising on *how* she would reach that goal, she was able to accomplish it.

Another key to compromise is to avoid being judgmental. If we pick up our grandchildren for church and never fail to chastise their parents for not going, we probably won't get the opportunity to take the children very often. When we are with our grandchildren and talk about faith or morality, we must avoid criticizing their parents' religious behavior. If we don't, Mom and Dad will understandably see this as an effort to undermine and judge them. Our children will already be defensive about turning away from their faith or from the family's values. They may see judgmentalism and legalism in our every comment or heavy sigh. We can't do anything about that, but we can let them know that even though we don't approve of the direction they are going, we still love them and welcome them into our home.

If we are to have any say in our grandchildren's moral and spiritual development, compromise is necessary. A hard-line attitude may end any opportunity to be a positive religious influence on our grandchildren.

## 5. Don't worry about the opinions of others.

Some of us let ourselves be guided by the prejudices and hang-ups of our friends, neighbors, and fellow church members. We like to believe that we aren't influenced by their attitudes, but the opinions of others do affect us. We need to acknowledge that fact, and to be on guard when grandparenting with a difference.

You may feel self-conscious the first time you bring your brain-injured grandson to church. A person like him may never have attended before. You may notice that you leave a trail of whispers behind you as you proudly lead him out to your car following the service. Creative, involved grandparents choose not to care. The choice comes down to this: Do I want my grandchild, regardless of his differences, to grow up knowing that I love him and that he is precious to me? Or am I going to let the narrow thinking of others—even my closest friends—keep me away from him?

If you are reading this book, you have already made your choice. You have decided that being an involved, creative grandparent is more important than golf, more important than board games with friends, and certainly more important than worrying about what the neighbors think. We must be careful, though. It is easier than we think to be controlled by the attitudes of others. It is possible that we are a little ashamed of the differences in our grandchildren. After all, you and I have our share of pride and prejudice. We have held these beliefs a very long time, and bigotry doesn't disappear with the birth of a grandchild who is "different." Inside we may still feel some shame.

The first step is to deal with those feelings immediately. We cannot pretend they don't exist. They will come out in subtle ways. Our real attitudes will show over time. Grandparents need to admit their struggle with the difference. Many of us live our whole lives acting as if we don't have any problems or prejudice, when in truth we have both. We will not be able to grandparent effectively until we acknowledge our irrational or sinful attitudes.

The second step is to seek God's help in renewing our thinking. We need His help to keep our minds free of bigotry, prejudice, and embarrassment. Only God can cleanse us from sinful attitudes that we have nourished for many years.

Don't allow the ignorant attitudes of others to keep you from being the best grandparent you can be. Tell them how much you love your grandchild. Do it loudly and often. Let everyone hear and see your pride in your "different" grandchild and your pleasure at being with him or her. This will silence the whispers and do wonders for your grandchild and family. The more time others spend with you and your grandchild, the more they will learn about and accept differences. This can be a learning time for your friends and relatives as well.

## 6. Follow the biblical mandate to love one another.

Jesus himself set the best example for those of us who are struggling to grandparent with a difference. Sitting beside a well, He talked intimately with a woman of low moral character and of a different nationality. He didn't condemn her or chastise her; He loved her. His example is our mandate. Love your grandchildren and your children. Although life may fling some surprises at you, don't use them as an excuse to become angry and withdraw from your family. The Bible says we are to love one another, for love is from God (see 1 John 4:7). I know it's easier said than done, but you can do it—with God's help.

Ed and Jean sat in my (Jerry's) office with stony looks on their faces. They were angry at their eighteen-year-old daughter. She had announced to them the week before that she was pregnant, and that the father was a black man. Ed and Jean have many of the prejudices of white middle-class people of their generation, and they were shocked. The pregnancy was bad enough; in reality, it confirmed their worst fears. But the fact that the baby was going to be biracial upset them even more.

When he heard the news, Ed lost his temper at his daughter. He swore that he would kill the father. Jean ran sobbing into her bedroom, her dreams for her daughter demolished. Now Ed and Jean wanted to know what they should do. Their thinking was that they should have no contact with their daughter except to pressure her to give up the baby for adoption. They were disappointed and angry and obviously were not thinking clearly. I listened, and then told them they were wrong. I encouraged them to love their daughter through this difficult time. I counseled them to support their daughter even if she went against their wishes and kept the baby. I asked them to consider opening their hearts to this new life. They thanked me curtly and left, still angry. I didn't think would ever see them again. They came for my approval and left without it.

Eight months later, on a sunny afternoon, I was sitting at my desk counseling another couple when my secretary rang in. "Jerry, a couple out here really wants to see you." I responded, "I'm in the middle of something right now. Can't it wait?" "No, I think you are going to want to see this," she replied. I excused myself and went to see what was so important. I was greeted by the smiling faces of Ed and Jean. No, they weren't just smiling, they were grinning from ear to ear. In their arms they were holding their six-week-old grandson. And they were very proud of him. I looked into the blanket and there he was, brown eyes shining brightly.

"Thanks, Jerry. We were angry at you at first. You didn't tell us what we wanted to hear. But once we calmed down, we decided to take your advice. And look at our grandson. Isn't he the cutest, most beautiful boy you have ever seen?" Ed and Jean both began to weep, and I cried with them that afternoon. Mine were tears of joy. Seeing them with the beautiful baby, I saw the deep, real love of two grandparents for their grandson. This was creative grandparenting with what was, for them, a difference.

Are you struggling with differences? Don't give up. You *can* overcome the obstacles of different ethnic backgrounds or religious beliefs or lifestyles and come to embrace and cherish all that you learn from these differences. You *can* creatively grandparent a special-needs child. You *can* grandparent with a difference. And you can do it well if you remember and practice these six principles:

1. Learn to live with your children's choices.
2. Do not punish your grandchildren for your children's choices.
3. Accept your grandchildren the way they are.
4. Work for compromise.
5. Don't worry about the opinions of others.
6. Follow the biblical mandate to love one another.

How well are you doing with each principle above? Talk with a spouse or friend about your need to improve in these areas. Then pick the principle that needs immediate improvement and develop a plan for change. Ask God for wisdom and courage to do the right thing, and ask a spouse or friend to hold you accountable. Once you have addressed the most immediate need, move on to another principle and repeat the process. Be patient with yourself in this ongoing process, but start the process today. You will not regret it!

CHAPTER 10

# In Harmony

wish I could have started as a grandparent. You know, just sort of skipped over the whole parenting bit and begun by being a grandpa immediately. I guess the fact that you have to be a parent before you can be a grandparent proves that God has a sense of humor."

As we interviewed grandparents for this book, we heard comments like this again and again. That's because so many of us struggled as parents. We had "on-the-job" training. We had no textbook to parent our children. We often learned by trial and error. By the time we perfected our parenting, our children had grown.

Sometimes our children didn't turn out quite as we had hoped. Along the way they made detours that scared the daylights out of us. Our anger at what we perceived as our children's failings shamed us, and our shame made us even angrier. We doubted our parenting skills. "Am I doing it right? Is there a right way at all? If I don't do it right, how will they turn out?"

No doubt about it, parenting can be a tough job, one for which few first-time parents are prepared. We "take our medicine," and most of the time it tasted like castor oil. By contrast, grandparenting is like a slice of chocolate-chip cheesecake, easy to take and enjoyable to the very end. In addition, most of our grandparenting is part-time. We get to enjoy our grandchildren with little responsibility. When they get tired and difficult, we take them home to their parents. There was no such relief during the full-time commitment of parenting.

The joy we derive from grandparenting can cause us to ignore our children, the foundation for our relationship with our grandchildren. We must realize that our relationship with our adult children directly and profoundly influences our relationship with our beloved grandchildren. We can't pretend that nothing came before. Our past, lived in full view of our children, plays a large role in our grandparenting.

To grandparent effectively and creatively, therefore, we must have a healthy, strong, harmonious relationship with our children. Let's illustrate. Jim loves being a grandparent. He can't wait to be with his grandsons, ages seven, five, and three. Some might even say that he spoils those boys when they come to visit. However, if you suggest that to him, he would defend himself by pointing out that gets them only four times a year. Jim is not a long-distance grandparent. His grandsons live only twenty-five minutes away. But Jim and his daughter do not get along. She thought he was a lousy parent, and he thought she was an ungrateful kid. The bitterness between them grew after she moved out. They have not resolved the hurt and anger of the past. Jim sees his grandchildren only four times a year because that's all his daughter allows. He is miserable because he is not a bigger part of their lives. His poor relationship with his daughter diminishes his time and connection with his grandsons.

Grandparenting, especially the involved, creative grandparenting we've been advocating, is impossible without the support of your children. If you are at odds with your children, this may be the most important chapter you read. As we begin, you need to realize that rediscovering your children can be a painful process. But it can bring cleansing and healing. We hope you will realize the importance of this chapter title, "In Harmony," as you ponder the truths you are about to read. Take a deep breath and get ready for a long look back as we discuss creative grandparenting as it relates to you and your children.

## The Importance of Being in Harmony

We cannot overstate the effect your relationship with your children has on your grandparenting. In fact, your satisfaction as a grandparent depends on it. Two words sum up the reason for this: *access* and *attitude*.

### Access

Our children control our access to our grandchildren. We may envision them as the conduit to our grandchildren. If they choose not to let us see them, or if they restrict the amount of time we can spend with them, our lives will be less fulfilling, and so will our grandchildren's.

It doesn't take a nuclear physicist to figure out that creative grandparenting depends on access. Long-distance grandparents have to rely on their children for access through phone calls, cards, e-mail, and occasional visits. And when we live nearby, our children control the day-to-day events of our grandchildren's lives. Our children can encourage and welcome access or limit and deny access. It is up to them. Without their cooperation, access to our grandchildren may become impossible, or at least limited.

Alice and Mary are neighbors in a small town. Each has a five-year-old grandson. Alice's grandson lives thirty miles from her home. Mary's lives more than two hundred miles away, in a suburb of Chicago. Last summer Mary spent two full months with Jimmy. They went to Brookfield Zoo, the beach, and the Shedd Aquarium. They took the elevator to the top of the tallest building in the United States, the Sears Tower, recently renamed the Willis Tower, and had a great time together. Mary and her grandson created memories that will stay with them for the rest of their lives. They now eagerly anticipate each summer together.

Alice saw her grandson, Tony, for a total of ten hours last year. Why was Mary, the long-distance grandmother, able to spend so much more time with her grandson? Mary and her daughter had some struggles growing up but resolved these long ago, and now have a great relationship. Mary is in harmony with her daughter. They see each other often and get along well. Mary's daughter treasures her mother's relationship with her son. She knows how important it is for her son to spend time with his grandmother. So, she freely grants Mary access to Jimmy.

Alice and her son, however, are still struggling with the pain he caused her during his teenage years. He abused alcohol and drugs. Even though he's been clean for seven years,

Alice cannot forgive him and still doesn't trust him. Their troubled relationship is an enormous barrier to Alice's grand-parenting. During the summer, Alice repeatedly invites little Tony to her house, but she makes it a point to invite only her grandson, not her son. Hurt, he angrily tells his mother that if he is not welcome or good enough for her, neither is his son. Alice needs to forgive her son and restore that relationship to enjoy time with her grandson. She knows what to do, but blames her son and refuses to accept responsibility for her lack of forgiveness.

Some grandparents know why they have limited access to their grandchildren. They are well aware that barriers exist between them and their children, and they do everything they can to break down the barriers. They reach out, admit their past failures, and humbly ask for forgiveness. Yet their children are unwilling to reconcile.

Others don't know what happened to cause such a rift. They have searched their hearts and asked God to reveal their shortcomings, but they still wonder why their children are so distant, detached, or angry. They cry at nights because they are not allowed to contact or visit their grandchildren. When they ask, "What have I done?" or "What can I do?" they are met with a blank stare and silence, or "You know what you have done." As far as it depends on them, they have done everything they can to make peace with their children (see Romans 12:18). They wait patiently for God or their children to reveal further direction that could lead to restored relationships.

Peter and his wife, Laura, have not seen their three grand-children for three years. Something happened during the sale of Peter and his son Andy's business that angered Andy and subsequently caused deep resentment toward Peter. Peter has no idea what happened. He has tried to talk to Andy, only to be met with sullenness and silence. Andy has not allowed either of his parents access to their grandchildren. Gifts are returned unopened. Their grandchildren are growing up without them. Peter and Laura are frustrated and puzzled and heartbroken. They long for restoration with their son and a relationship with their grandchildren. They wait patiently and pray for insight and resolution.

Without a doubt, our children control access to our grandchildren. When we keep our relationship with our children healthy, working hard to clear up old issues and deal quickly and reasonably with current problems, usually access to our grandchildren will be offered. Sometimes this requires forgiveness on our part; sometimes it requires admission of wrongdoing and a request for forgiveness. Often it requires humility. Don't wait for your children to come to you to reconcile. You may wait years, and while you wait, you lose precious time with your growing grandchildren. Take responsibility, do the right thing, and restore the relationship. Work hard toward harmonious relationships with your children.

### Attitude

Our children also control our grandchildren's attitude toward us. If our children often disagree with us and express that disagreement to their children, they will influence our grandchildren's attitude toward us. If our children regard us with suspicion and mistrust, our grandchildren will probably feel the same way. If our children trust us and speak highly of us to their children, our grandchildren will also trust us and hold us in high esteem.

The parental power to determine attitudes may be even more important than access. As grandparents, we can sometimes win the right to see our grandchildren, even if it means going to court. But we cannot dictate the attitudes our children have toward us, nor control what our children say about us to our grandchildren. Some parents continually disparage their parents, or one set of parents, to the grandchildren. These impressionable young minds become filled with negative images of Grandma and Grandpa. Your children and their spouses have great power in directing your grandchildren's affections.

When we recognize the power our children have over our relationships with our grandchildren, we may respond in one of two unproductive ways. We may become angry and defensive, or we may become too eager to please our children. These behaviors will not help our cause as creative grandparents. One parent said to me, "The only reason my mother is nice to me is because she's afraid that if she treats me like she always has, I won't let her see the children. She was always sharp-tongued and critical. Now she's so icky sweet I can't stand it!"

Your children are not stupid. They will see right through your behavior to your motives. If your relationship with your son has been difficult in the past, and following the arrival of a new grandchild you suddenly try to dive into his life as if nothing has happened, he will know what you're up to. He will still possess his anger and resentment toward you from the past. We can't start the relationship with our children brand-new, forgetting all that has gone on before, just because we now have a grandchild.

The onset of grandparenting, however, does present a wonderful opportunity to improve our relationships with our adult children. The birth of a grandchild can remind us that we need to take care of business with our children, that we need to right some wrongs. We cannot afford to wait for our children to move toward us. We need to be responsible and obedient to Scripture, which tells us to go to our brother if we know he has something against us, to settle matters quickly and reconcile with him (Matthew 5:23–24). God always honors obedience and expects obedience from His children. God tells His people, the Israelites, "Those who honor Me I will honor" (1 Samuel 2:30). Bill, a forty-seven-year-old grandparent, understands and illustrates the scriptural truth:

> Dad and I didn't get along very well while I was in high school and college. In fact, that's putting it mildly. I always felt like Dad expected too much of me. I had to be a great athlete. I had to get straight As in school. I felt like I had to be the perfect Christian. I just couldn't do it all. I had my own ideas about who I should be and what I wanted to accomplish.
>
> I spent a lot of time rebelling against my dad, and in a lot of ways I acted like a jerk to him. You know, just mean whenever I thought I could get away with it. Over the years our relationship has kind of steadied out, with him tolerating me and me not yelling at him. But we really had never come to terms with our past. I didn't think it was possible or even necessary.
>
> That is, until my daughter was born. She is my parents' first grandchild. It was weird, but as I stood over Marissa's crib, I began to understand my father. I realized that the hopes and fears I have for my daughter are similar to those my dad had for me. And watching him

with Marissa, I see a side of him, a gentleness, that I had never seen before. I went to my dad the other day, and for the first time in years, I asked him for advice. I thought he was going to fall over! But a smile came over his face and we talked, I mean really talked, for the first time in ten years.

Wise, creative grandparents do not see their children as obstacles to their happiness, but as people who need love, patient understanding, and support. Some grandparents love their grandchildren at the expense of their children. It is an easy trap to fall into, especially if they have struggled with their feelings about their adult children. They may see them as no longer needing the approval of their parents. Nothing could be further from the truth. Many, if not most, of our adult children still crave the approval of their parents, even into midlife. Why not discover anew their qualities, and let them know how much you appreciate them.

So far we have assumed that the relationship between grandparents and parents is not particularly good. Now we address the other side. Grandparents who enjoy the love, trust, and respect of their children are much more likely to receive those same feelings from their grandchildren. My appointed role of "best grandfather in the world" comes not only from the time I spend with my grandkids, but also from the positive spin my children give to me and my actions as they discuss them with their children. My great relationship with my grandkids began with a great relationship with my two boys. In a sense I am just repeating, with more maturity, sometimes more risk, and certainly more money, the activities I enjoyed earlier with my children. I'm just a bit better at it today than I was as a young parent. Creative grandparenting seems so much easier than parenting, and in many ways it is much more fun.

## Pitfalls to Avoid

Because we know how important our children are to our creative grandparenting opportunities, we must treat our children with love and respect, especially in front of our grandchildren. Sadly, that does not always happen. Sometimes we say the wrong things or do stupid things that threaten the relationship with our children, poisoning their attitudes and causing them to restrict the time allowed with our grandchildren. A few examples of these missteps follow.

### Parenting Your Grandchildren

Nothing upsets your children more than when you step into their role. You're the grandparent. That's your role. Enjoy it. Don't become the parent; that is the job of your kids. Don't rob them of their responsibility by stepping in to interfere with their discipline. Don't tell your grandkids that you disagree with their parents' style of parenting or the discipline they mete out. You may have your opinions and good ideas for proper parenting, but keep them to yourself to stay in harmony with your children. Read more about interference in chapter 6.

### Usurping Your Children's Authority

Another way to say a quick good-bye to harmonious relationships with your children is to violate their authority. If they tell you that their children are not allowed to have a snack before dinner or chocolates before bedtime, ignore the parents' wishes and buy your grandchildren ice cream cones or give them treats. After all, you and I are the real grown-ups, right? We know better than our children. So what if the kids are hyper because of the caffeine in the chocolates? So what if they don't finish their dinner? After all, don't grandparents have the right to spoil their grandchildren? What the parents don't know won't hurt them.

Better to honor the parents' wishes and stay in harmony with your children. Your grandchildren will survive without that snack, and you will show your support for their parents.

### Criticizing Your Children Publicly

If parenting your grandchildren or usurping their parents' authority isn't enough to anger your children, then criticizing them in front of others is sure to do the trick. You don't have to be obnoxious about it; just let it be known that you believe they have a lot to learn as parents. Give them the impression that you have all the answers. The key here is to do it in front of their friends or, even better, in front of the children. Do as much as you can to undermine their credibility with your grandchildren. "Now, son, I can't believe you let the children go outside in weather like this without their hats. And look at their coats! How long has it been since they were washed? They really need replacing. If you don't have the money for new coats, I'll buy them for the kids." A few sentences like the above and you will soon be out of harmony with your children

Maybe your children don't parent like you do, or have the same expectations for your grandchildren as you do. Give them the right to do their job they way they deem fit, and keep your mouth shut. In the long run your grandchildren will survive, and even thrive, under the supervision of their parents. There is more than one way (your way) to parent effectively. Don't criticize their way. It is more important for you as grandparents to stay in harmony with your kids. They control access and attitude. Don't forget this important truth.

### One-upping Your Children

A fourth good way to antagonize your children is to help them see how much more you love their children than they do. Of course, it might be necessary to spend a little money to bribe your grandchildren with candy, clothes, and toys. Take a few months to prepare for the big moment. Finally it comes. You trot the grandchildren into the living room before a large family gathering and ask with a loud voice, "Now who do you children love best, Mom or Grandma?" Parents are always delighted when their recently bribed children point to Grandma.

In this case, Grandma probably has her own issues to need this kind of approval. It is enough just to love and be loved by our grandchildren. We don't need to publicly compare our love with that of our children. A parent's love is different from a grandparent's love. A grandparent's love usually has little responsibility attached. It is easier and not to be compared with a parent's love. Parents responsibly attend to a child's needs and desires for up to twenty years or more.

The more responsible thing for this grandmother to do would be to point out the depth of her children's love for their children, and tell the children how fortunate they are to have experienced their parents' love and care.

### Keeping the Past Alive

Another way to alienate your children is to remind them about how bad they were to you when they were children.

Constantly remind them of their past failures. Never let them forget how much they hurt you or disappointed you. Imply that your life would have been so much easier without them. Tell them of the pain they brought into your life.

This will assure you of limited access to your grandchildren. Your children will avoid you like the plague. After all, who wants to continually hear of their failures and be told that they are a disappointment? You may be able to live with alienation from your children, but will you be able to live without access to your grandchildren? Better to forgive and forget, move on, and enjoy your children and your grandchildren. Stay in harmony with your children to enjoy access to your grandchildren.

## The Road to Reconciliation

In strained relationships, the tendency is to blame the other person for our feelings toward him or her. Especially in parent-child relationships, we tell ourselves we did our best and we tried our hardest to raise our child well. We sincerely believe it isn't our fault that our children misread our intentions or were hurt by our expectations. They should have known how we really felt.

If we continue to point the finger of blame and responsibility at them, we will never achieve reconciliation. At best we can hope for an uneasy truce, forced on us by our impressionable grandchildren. But it does not have to be that way! The sooner we realize that we cannot control the actions of our children, and the sooner we accept responsibility for our part in the conflict and the healing, the sooner we'll be able to get on with the business of creative grandparenting.

As parents and grandparents intent on rebuilding our relationships with our children and forging strong relationship with our grandchildren, it's time to close out all outstanding accounts. It's time to balance the books and slam the covers of that dusty old ledger together with a resounding thump!

In the movie *Home Alone,* eight-year-old Kevin finds himself sitting in church beside his elderly neighbor, a bedraggled old man who is the subject of frightening rumors among the neighborhood children. The man is there during a Christmas choir rehearsal because he knows he wouldn't be welcome during the performance. Years before, he and his son had a longstanding grievance that had erupted into harsh words and flailing fists. The old man was not allowed to see his beautiful granddaughter, so he sneaked in when he wouldn't be noticed. Sensing his anguish and pain, Kevin asked him a simple question, "Why don't you just go to your son and tell him you're sorry?" The old man mumbled that it wasn't that simple and sidled away.

The first step on the road to reconciliation really is that simple. To begin the process of reconciliation, follow young Kevin's sage advice and *go to your children.* This first step will probably be the most difficult. It takes humility and courage to lose face. The producers of *Home Alone* probably did not know it, but they were giving biblical advice. According to Matthew 18:15, the first step to reconciliation is to go to the person one-on-one. And Matthew 5:23–24 says that if you know someone has something against you, go to that person and reconcile before you offer your gifts to the Lord.

The Scriptures are clear: go to your children. Go, even if you feel they have done you wrong. Go, even if it means setting aside your pride. Go, even if you are certain they are more to blame than you are. Your relationship with them, and with your precious grandchildren, is far more important than a stubborn question of who did what to whom. Take the first step toward reconciliation. Go to your children.

When you go, take the next step and *acknowledge past mistakes*. Now is the time to say, "I was wrong. I realize it now. I am sorry." Now is the time to admit that you failed at times. Now is the time to agree that you sometimes did the wrong thing. Remind them that parenting is hard. They should begin to understand, because now they are parents too.

When we have come this far, we might expect our children to make a big move toward us. Don't. After all, it may have taken you ten years to figure out where you went wrong. It may take them another ten to see where they were wrong. Don't be hurt if, when you acknowledge your mistakes, they don't rush to you with open arms and tearful celebration. Deep hurts take a long time to heal. By taking these two steps to begin the healing process, you're doing the right thing.

Let your children know that in admitting your failures, you are not expecting anything in return. This is not a game of quid pro quo. Your painful disclosure and apology may be met with suspicion or indifference. That's okay. You have done your part. "He who conceals his sins does not prosper, but whoever confesses and renounces them finds mercy" (Proverbs 28:13 NIV). This principle applies to us as parents. We may not feel we have sinned, but we know that we have failed. Admit it, and ask for mercy. Forget about justice. God will take care of that. Go to your children with a gentle spirit and acknowledge your past mistakes.

The third step to reconciliation is to *accept God's forgiveness*. We often beat ourselves up for past mistakes. The past is gone. Some things simply cannot be undone. We can't go back twenty years and spend more time with our children. We can't take back angry words spoken long ago. We can't call back a hand loosed in anger. It's even too late for deep regrets.

Know that God has forgiven all your failings, all your mistakes, all your sins. Because you have acknowledged your sins and failures and repented, God has reached down and touched you with His loving, forgiving hand. In Jesus Christ you have been forgiven.

Mary is gloomy all the time. She looks back on her fifty-nine years with regret and longing. She was not a very good parent. She was impatient, demanding, and quick to become angry. She screamed terrible words at her children. As a result, her relationships with her adult children are very poor. Mary has tried to forget the past, but it won't go away. She knows she was not a very good mom, yet she wants a chance to be a good grandparent. Her children are learning to forgive her, and they are rediscovering one another. But Mary is difficult to be around because she will not forgive herself. She dwells on her past failings constantly. It seems to be all she thinks about. She is missing her grandchildren's wonder years because she will not let herself accept the loving forgiveness of God. Mary needs to remember Paul's words to the Corinthians: "If anyone is in Christ, he is a new creation; the old has gone, the new has come!" (2 Corinthians 5:17 NIV).

## If You Need Help Reconciling

In her book, *Traits of a Healthy Family,* Delores Curran points out healthy families are not afraid to ask for help. When the problems between you and your children are so deep and the misunderstandings so pronounced that you no longer feel capable of resolving the conflict, don't give up. Ask for help. When we are confronted by obstacles that seem insurmountable, the answer is to look outside of ourselves for assistance.

The first place we should turn is often our last resort. Don't wait until it's too late to ask God to intervene in your relationships with your children. He is our best resource! The Bible speaks repeatedly of the power of prayer. Seek reconciliation by going to your children, acknowledging past mistakes, and accepting God's forgiveness. Make prayer an important part of the process. Ask God for help.

Ask other family members for help. Don't let them gang up on your son or daughter, but consider using them as an intermediary. If every discussion between you and your daughter turns ugly, perhaps your son can be a calming influence. Family members can be valuable resources in bringing reconciliation to relationships within the family.

You might also want to consider your pastor or church as a source of help. Pastors and church friends can be a source of tremendous encouragement to you. They will pat you on the back for going down the difficult path of reconciliation, hug you when things don't go well, and rejoice with you when the relationship is restored. The key is to let someone know what is going on. Be wise, of course, and discreet. Tell trusted church people the truth and let them know you need their support and prayers. You cannot do it alone, and you don't have to. Don't let shame or embarrassment rob you of the loving, confidential support of your pastor and friends.

Finally, if you cannot find reconciliation any other way, look to a trained family counselor for help. He or she can help you understand your past and how it has affected your parenting. The counselor can put your present relationships in perspective. A good counselor can give you wise insight and help you form a plan for working through the hurts and pain of the past to reconcile with your children.

## Rethinking the Process

The single biggest factor in your grandparenting career is your relationship with your children. Don't minimize the relationship's importance. Take the lead. Be proactive. Look for ways to improve your children's attitudes toward you. Look for opportunities to build up and help your children. Remember, a parent's relationship with his or her adult children does not take care of itself. Tend that relationship, not only because you should and want to, but knowing that your grandparenting depends on it. Take the risks involved to reconcile with your children. Don't let pride stand in your way. Your grandchildren need you. Do it for them, for yourself, and for the Lord.

"Live in harmony with one another. Do not be proud . . . If it is possible, as far as it depends on you, live at peace with everyone. Do not take revenge, my friends . . . Do not be overcome by evil, but overcome evil with good" (Romans 12:16–21 NIV).

# CHAPTER 11

## Back to Parenting

Bob and Joyce were excited and ready to begin their retirement adventure. They had raised their family and worked hard, and now they looked forward to enjoying the fruit of their labors. They had purchased an SUV and were ready to purchase a travel trailer when a phone call from a school social worker changed everything.

The social worker informed them that their grandson, twelve-year-old Christopher, had been observed taking food from the garbage. The Department of Social Services investigated and removed him from his home immediately. Now Chris's options were limited to a foster home or living with his grandparents. "We didn't want our grandson to live with strangers," Bob and Joyce said. They quickly agreed to take Christopher.

Bob and Joyce were unprepared for the naked truth of this young man's life. He came to them malnourished with shoes two sizes too small and few clothes. Whenever they moved their hands suddenly, he would duck his head. "Chris arrived anxious, skinny, afraid, abused, and with no friends," said Joyce.

After divorcing Chris's biological mom, their son had married a woman who did not accept Christopher. He was often locked in his room and had to sneak food to eat. Chris hid the situation well. When clearing the table, which was his job, he would wrap table scraps in tinfoil and retrieve them from the garbage can later.

Chris's father and stepmom had limited the amount of time Chris spent with Bob and Joyce. Although they had some concerns that life was hard for Chris, never did they realize the extent of his abuse. Their hearts broke as Chris revealed more and more about life with his dad and stepmom. Bob and Joyce had to work through their emotions. They struggled with their own son not caring for his child, and with their former daughter-in-law who was imprisoned for attempting to kill their grandson when he was only three years old.

Now Bob and Joyce love and care for their precious grandson as though he were their own child. They encourage him, teach him, and clothe him. During mealtimes, they listen carefully to Chris and tell him how creative and how strong he was to survive. They tell him how proud they are of him. Chris is now flourishing in his new home.

Grandparents who are "back to parenting" may have looked forward to their role of "loving and leaving" their grandchildren—spoiling and pleasing them, adoring them, and then bringing them back to mom and dad. Now they find themselves parenting instead of grandparenting, which is much less fun and a whole lot more work. They are responsible for full-time child care, including the discipline and education of their grandchildren. This is not the kind of grandparenting they expected or dreamed about.

Most grandparents do not choose to go back to parenting. A family crisis precipitates this new role, such as the absence, death, or incarceration of the parent(s), parental substance abuse, mental or physical illness, or teenage pregnancy. According to researcher Dorothy Ruiz, ninety percent of the nearly one hundred thousand women in U.S. prisons are single mothers with children under eighteen years of age. Although other relatives may provide care for these children, the burden of child care falls upon the grandmother more than 50 percent of the time.

According to data from the U.S. census of 2000, the number of children living with their grandparents increased by 53 percent between 1990 and 1998. Today more than 2.4 million homes in the U.S. are headed by grandparents who have primary responsibility for one or more of their grandchildren. One million of these homes have only a grandmother and 150,000 have only a grandfather. (The rest of the homes have both grandparents.) Fifty-five percent of these grandmothers and 47 percent of the grandfathers are under the age of fifty-five. The average income for homes with only a grandmother present is $19,750. That changes drastically when the grandfather is also present, to $61,632. More than 20 percent of these grandparents have cared for their grandchildren for more than five years and do not see an end in sight.

For some grandparents, going back to parenting is stressful, unwelcome, and burdensome. For others, it is a special time with their grandchildren that brings closeness, enjoyment, and fulfillment. The stress grandparents feel has to do with choice, perception, and resources. Grandparents who willingly made the choice to parent their grandchildren often experience greater enjoyment and fulfillment than those who felt they were the only option their grandchildren had left. These grandparents felt obligated to go back to parenting, often without the financial, emotional, and physical resources necessary for the task. When grandparents perceive going back to parenting as a wonderful opportunity to be with and positively influence their grandchildren, they experience closeness and satisfaction in their new role. Our challenge for those of you who are back to parenting is to look at full-time caregiving as a grand opportunity to be a creative grandparent, loving and nurturing a new generation.

## Choices, Satisfaction, and Stress

Grandmothers who provide full-time care for their grandchildren report significantly lower levels of grandparenting and life satisfaction than either part-time caregiving grandmothers or non-caregiving grandmothers. Researchers attribute this lower satisfaction to a stressful, nonnormative life event that was not really a choice, or was an unwelcome choice, for the grandmothers.

We tend to make choices that lead to our satisfaction and fulfillment. Yet when we become caregivers to our grandchildren, we must set aside many of our needs and desires. William Glasser, in his book *Choice Theory*, lists five basic needs for each human being: (1) the need for belonging or being connected in a relationship with others; (2) the need to have some type of control over our lives; (3) the need to pursue what interests us; (4) the need for enjoyment; and (5) the desire to satisfy physiological needs necessary for survival. Going back to parenting threatens at least three of the above personal needs, and brings inner conflict to grandparents. One grandparent said, "We used to caravan for about nine months of the year. Now the caravan's gone, the car's gone, and we've changed our lifestyle completely to look after our grandchild. Sometimes I regret that, but sometimes I still wouldn't go back to it."

Another grandfather said, "I didn't feel I was able to care for a small child this late in life, but we didn't have any choice. We are all Jeremy has left. What will happen to him if we don't care for him? He has no one else." "We would rather have our grandson with us than for him to go to a foster home, or stay in an unsafe place," said another grandparent.

Let's look at two couples facing the same caregiving responsibility. Mary and Jim are financially well off, in good physical health, well-educated, and emotionally close to their grandchildren. They have support from friends and family, a strong faith, and a caring church family. They have good problem-solving and communication skills, and are willing to go back to parenting. Mary and Jim do not perceive their situation as stressful, but see it as an opportunity to help their family and be with their grandchildren at a difficult time. They gladly changed their lifestyle to serve and preserve their family. Mary and Jim would likely report high levels of satisfaction with their new roles as full-time caregivers.

Bill and Sandra are barely getting by financially, in failing health, not well-educated, and somewhat distant from their grandchildren. They have little support from friends, relatives, or church family. They have poor problem-solving and communication skills and have difficulty trusting God. For

Bill and Sandra, going back to parenting is stressful and not at all desired. They struggle with resentment because of the responsibilities cast upon them by their child. They still try to be the best caregivers possible, but feel exploited by their child. Bill and Sandra are candidates for decreased physical health and increased depression, which could lead to additional stress and personal or family crisis.

According to family scholar Reuben Hill, stressors lead to crises when we have limited resources and a negative perception of the stressor. In other words, the more we perceive parenting our grandchildren as fulfilling, satisfying, and enjoyable, the less we experience stress and the possibility of moving into crisis. Further, when we have access to necessary resources, we will have a more positive perception of parenting our grandchildren, and we will avert additional stress and crises.

Our resources are both external and internal. External resources include finances, education, living space, insurance, respite care, social support, and physical health. Our internal resources include faith, personal coping skills, problem-solving abilities, and psychological health and maturity. When these resources are present, we will perceive going back to parenting as positive and satisfying. When they are absent, we will perceive parenting our grandchildren as stressful and undesired. If resources are not available over a long period of time, we may move into a crisis like a breakdown in our physical or mental health.

## Challenges

What are the stressors involved in parenting grandchildren? Grandparents face personal challenges, family challenges, and challenges from the grandchildren themselves. All of these can add considerable stress to grandparents' lives at a time when grandparents normally settle down with fewer responsibilities to enjoy their later years.

### Personal Challenges

Families today are having children later in life, which means grandparents may be older also. Some of these grandparents are frail and less physically able to care for their grandchildren or keep up with them. These grandparents may feel guilty for not being able to participate in physical activities that benefit their grandchildren. One sixty-eight-year-old grandmother said, "When I was young, I had much more energy to do things with my kids. Now I am old and don't have the energy to go places with my granddaughter. She wants to go and I would love to go with her, but I just don't have the energy."

Twelve-year-old Andy loves to hike in the mountains where he lives with his grandparents, David and Sandy. Because hiking is Andy's favorite thing to do, his grandfather continues to go with him, but it is becoming increasingly difficult for David due to his deteriorating knees. He takes pain relievers before and after each hike. David has been reluctant to tell Andy that he can no longer hike because he doesn't want to disappoint his grandson. Andy's father used to hike with him, but he is no longer present in Andy's life. His mom is in and out of a drug rehab facility and has been unable to care for her son.

Some grandparents struggle with daily tasks such as cooking, cleaning, and child care. These tasks may be new to grandfathers who never had responsibility for these chores before, and these men may feel inadequate and frustrated at their own inability. Traditional grandfathers may feel that these jobs are a woman's responsibility.

Often grandparents do not feel adequately educated for the task of helping their grandchildren with schoolwork, especially with subjects grandparents took forty or fifty years ago, or subjects that are unfamiliar to them. They feel helpless and insufficient for these tasks. Frustration and stress occur because grandparents know that the subjects are important for their grandchildren's success in school and later in life. One or both grandparents lack a high school diploma for one-third of children living with grandparents.

More than 60 percent of back-to-parenting grandparents are still in the workforce. The roles of grandparent, parent, employee, and spouse at times are demanding and conflict with one another. Our grandkids need us, our kids need us, our employer still expects us to do our job, and our spouse wants more time with us. Carol and Carl are in a second marriage and provide primary care for Carol's five year-old granddaughter, Rachel. Carl works full-time in a high-stress job, and Carol works part-time, while also caring for her two teenage sons from her previous marriage. She is also taking a night class in college, trying to finish a bachelor's degree.

Carl is okay with the idea of caring for her granddaughter and supports Carol's plan to finish college, but he is unable to contribute much to the task of parenting because of his responsibilities at work. Also, he is often gone fishing with his friends on weekends. When he is home, he wants more time with Carol, but she is too tired to do anything with him. This means additional stress on the marriage and on Carol, who believes that she is contributing more than her husband. She continually resists his sexual advances because of her resentment and fatigue. Periodically, Carl threatens separation or divorce if things don't change. At times Carol wonders if the additional challenge of parenting a grandchild is worth it. But her granddaughter needs her. There is no one else.

Grandparents who go back to parenting are also challenged financially. With more mouths to feed and bodies to care for, grandparents face rising expenses, often when they are on fixed incomes. Compared to other households, grandparent-grandchild households are more likely to receive public assistance and less likely to have health insurance. According to the 2000 Census, the poverty rate for grandparent-grandchild households is 27 percent, compared to 19 percent for parent-child households. Two-thirds of households with only a grandmother raising grandchildren are poor. Having limited funds bothers these grandmothers who want to care for their grandchildren, meet their needs, and give them a good life. They are disappointed when their financial situation hinders their efforts to adequately provide for their grandchildren.

Fifteen-year-old Keisha is very involved with her church youth group and wants to attend every special event and outing, some of which cost more than her caregiver grandmother can afford. Keisha has already lost both of her parents, one to an accidental death and the other to incarceration. All her friends are at church. It's hard for her grandmother to say no to her when she wants her to participate in these activities and be with her friends. She refuses to ask for financial help from people at church. Instead, Keisha's grandmother gives up one of her medications so she can pay for her granddaughter's outings and activities.

Many custody and caregiving arrangements between family members are informal, which means grandparents receive little or no financial or social services support or direction. For some, this is not a problem, but for many fixed-income grandparents, this leads to financial strain and a stretched budget. It can mean a struggle for grandparents to provide for themselves and their grandchildren. It also means lost opportunities for grandparents to enjoy their later adult years, such as having to postpone or cancel travel and retirement plans.

### Family Challenges

In addition to personal and financial challenges are family challenges. Sometimes younger grandparents also care for their adolescent children, elderly parents, a chronically ill child, or a sick spouse. These grandparents often resent the addition of child-care responsibilities, especially parenting their children's children. They struggle with their children's choices that led them to abandon or give up their children. They may be angry at their children for what they have done or have failed to do, yet they love their grandchildren and cannot bear to see them suffer because of their parents' mistakes and problems. They feel responsible to do what they can to alleviate the suffering of their grandchildren.

Back-to-parenting grandparents often struggle with the loss of their own children to death, disease, disablement, substance abuse, or incarceration. They are grieving these losses while accepting additional responsibilities of caring for their grandchildren. Some grandparents are concerned that their grandchildren are growing up in an unsafe place, and they want to protect them, even if that means providing for them. As they adopt new caregiving roles, the stressors from their everyday lives continue.

## Grandchildren's Challenges

Often grandchildren enter a caregiving arrangement because of loss. A parent may have died or been imprisoned or abandoned the child. The child's losses complicate the adjustment to living with grandparents, and may result in acting out. Studies show that children of full-time caregiving grandparents have more behavioral problems than other children. Grandchildren often bring with them the behavioral problems associated with poor parenting, drug abuse, and neglect at home. Behavioral issues put an additional burden on grandparents, as do concerns about the losses their grandkids are experiencing. Grandchildren who are uprooted from their parents' home lose their parents, their home, and often their friends, especially if they had to move to another city or school system.

Researcher Patricia Gibson shares the story of sixty-five-year-old Grandmother Birch, who is a retired widow. She has been caring for her twelve-year-old grandson for two years, and is well aware of the challenges he faces. "He is a loner, he has just one friend and he misses his mom and dad so much. He is hurting inside . . . I can teach him a lot of things, but lots of things I can't teach him well." She expresses her concern for her grandson and for her gender limitations in caring for him: "He needs a male figure to teach him how to be a man. He has got to go out one day and be a man, the head of his family."

Many challenges face grandparents when they go back to parenting. Most of these can be overcome, but they take a physical, emotional, and financial toll on grandparents. While grandparents believe that they are needed by their grandchildren and find purpose in filling a necessary role, they often experience additional stress, burden, and disappointment as they raise their grandchildren.

Although some grandparents face challenges when they assume the role of parenting grandchildren, somehow they find the strength to continue and experience a sense of satisfaction as they go back to parenting. For them, this new role brings tremendous enjoyment and fulfillment.

## Enjoyment and Fulfillment

Despite the challenges, many grandparents report that going back to parenting has been a positive experience. More than 40 percent of full-time caregiving grandparents are retired, with time to parent that they did not have when they were parenting their own children. Some single parents had to work more than one job and found it difficult to give their children the time and attention they felt their children needed. Now as grandparents, they can spend the time necessary to be the parents that they wanted to be earlier, when time was at a premium.

Grandparents are often more relaxed than parents and make fewer demands on children. They have sorted out what is really important and what is not. They don't argue with their grandchildren over things that don't matter. A little dust or spilled milk isn't a big deal. They just want to love and care for their grandchildren. Some believe that going back to parenting is a second chance to parent that allows them to correct the mistakes they made the first time.

Grandparents report that they laugh more with their grandchildren than they did while parenting their children. One grandparent said, "I was too strict with my children, always thinking that I had to be the perfect parent." Some grandparents believe that they were too serious as parents. Now a mistake is tolerated, they are more relaxed, and they have more fun with their grandchildren.

These grandparents also report more confidence and maturity dealing with children and various problems. When they were young parents, they were learning how to parent on the job. Now with the wisdom gained by experience, parenting seems much easier, less stressful, and more enjoyable. One grandmother said, "Raising my grandchildren is special, and I really enjoy my time with them."

Many grandparents who go back to parenting report greater life satisfaction and confidence that they're positively influencing future generations. These grandparents have new purpose in life, which gives them renewed energy for the task of parenting. Grandchildren who are living with someone who loves them and is willing to raise them gives them great advantages over children in some alternate family or foster situations.

## Making "Back to Parenting" a Positive Experience

How can you be one of the fulfilled grandparents who enjoys being a full-time caregiver for your grandchildren? The following suggestions will help you enjoy being back to parenting with your grandchildren.

*Maintain a positive outlook.* When grandparents see parenting their grandchildren as an opportunity versus an obligation, they will be more positive about the experience. The experience will become a blessing rather than a burden. Another way to view being back to parenting is as an appointment from God for this time in your life. Remember Mordecai's words to Queen Esther, when he asked her to go to the king to ask for mercy for God's people, Israel? After Haman's attempt to eradicate the entire nation, Mordecai said to the Queen, "Who knows but that you have come to royal position for such a time as this?" (Esther 4:14 NIV).

While going back to parenting may not seem to be a "royal" position, it is a privileged position. When parenting grandchildren is seen as an appointment from God "for such a time as this," you will not feel as disappointed with your children or disappointed by personal losses incurred because of going back to parenting. You may not be happy with your children because of their neglect, or actions, but you will be more focused on the blessings you are experiencing with your grandchildren than on any losses you have incurred. View being back to parenting as a blessing rather than a burden, an opportunity rather than an obligation.

Perception of your situation often determines outcome. You will not only avert a crisis, but your stress will likely decrease and you will be able to enjoy your wonderful grandkids once again. Thank God daily for their presence and your opportunity to be with them. Ask God for strength and wisdom for each day. Love and enjoy them always. Look at your situation positively and be grateful for the opportunity to care for your grandchildren.

*Take one day at a time.* Jesus gave us this advice: "Do not worry about tomorrow, for tomorrow will worry about itself. Each day has enough trouble of its own" (Matthew 6:34 NIV).

Most of us are easily overwhelmed when we look too far into the future. When we think about all the things we need to do in the weeks and months ahead, we begin to worry. God never intended for us to take on the worries of tomorrow today. It would be easy, for instance, for grandparents who are parenting younger grandkids to think about parenting them when they become teenagers. Or they may worry about their own declining physical abilities and stamina as they try to keep up with active adolescents. They may worry about how their grandchildren will turn out, or question their ability to parent a particular grandchild. The advice of Jesus still stands. Take one day at a time. Focus on the present, not on the future. Live each day to the fullest with your grandchildren. You will experience more joy and less stress as a back-to-parenting grandparent.

*Care for yourself.* Often caregivers are so concerned about caring for others that they don't take time to care for themselves. Grandparents who are back to parenting care deeply about their grandchildren. That's why they have invited them to live in their home. They willingly sacrifice for them, extending themselves financially, emotionally, and physically, sometimes to their very limit.

Many back-to-parenting grandparents are reluctant to take a vacation, or a break from parenting. They fail to take time to be with friends and relatives. They forgo fun times and don't take time for relaxation and refreshment. These committed grandparents desire the best for their grandchildren. However, their lifestyle is a recipe for disaster, both for them and their grandchildren. Burned-out grandparents are not good parents. They will struggle physically, emotionally, and spiritually. They may become discouraged, depressed, and bitter. They lose their joy and enthusiasm. Grandchildren will notice a change in their attitudes and actions, and may respond with negative behavior, which in turn brings more stress upon grandparents.

If you are a creative, involved grandparent who is back to parenting, you need to take time to "smell the roses" as you walk through the garden of life with your grandchildren by your side. Enjoy the days and moments God has given you, take vacations, and do things just for fun. Take time away from parenting your grandchildren to be with friends. Take time to care for yourself, and make this a priority—do this first, not last. When you practice caring for yourself you will become a healthier person and a better equipped grandparent who enjoys being back to parenting. Before commercial airplanes leave the ground, flight attendants remind passengers of proper procedure for oxygen masks. They explain that masks will come down from above the seats if oxygen is required. Parents are told to place the mask over their own mouth and nose first, before caring for their children. The implication is clear: take care of yourself first, so you will be able to care for others later.

*Recognize your capabilities.* Many grandparents feel inadequate for the task of parenting, especially older grandparents. Their own children have been out of the house for many years. These grandparents need to remember that their years of experience and resulting wisdom and maturity are great resources for being back to parenting. These resources are likely greater than most parents possess. Don't feel bad or inadequate if you don't possess all of the skills and education you think you need to be a twenty-first-century parent. Do the best you can with your experience, maturity, and wisdom gained throughout your many years. Be reminded that, for the Christian, our adequacy comes from above. Learn to trust God for results when you begin to doubt your abilities and wonder how your grandchildren will turn out. Focus on your capabilities, rather than on your perceived inabilities.

*Ask for help when needed.* Healthy families ask for help when needed. Don't assume that others know your needs. Develop a social support system of friends, relatives, family members, neighbors, and church family. Become aware of and use community resources like grandparent/parent support groups, school counselors, tutors, church pastoral staff, social service agencies, mental health organizations, and family therapists. Connect with a social worker who is knowledgeable about available services in your community. Periodically chat with a pastor or family counselor for insight and encouragement for the challenging task that you have undertaken. Strengthen your relationship with friends and relatives. Develop friendships with people at your church. They may become your best resources. Don't forget to ask God for wisdom and direction (James 1:5). Also ask God to direct you to others who can help. Then accept the help when it is offered.

Remember the grandparents we talked about at the beginning of this chapter, Bob and Joyce? They readily accepted help from others. Most weekends their grandson, Christopher, spent time with another family from their church. This family had children about the same age as Chris. They became his siblings, young people with whom he could identify and connect. For nearly six years, Chris spent most weekends with the family. When they went camping, Chris went with them. When they celebrated special occasions, Chris was there too. When Chris needed help with schoolwork, the parents assisted.

Chris became an important part of their family. They loved him as their own. The parents call Chris their "weekend son." Grandparents Bob and Joyce told us how helpful this family has been, how their involvement with Chris has made their job so much easier. Creative grandparents need to ask for help and accept that help when it is offered. Asking for help when needed will relieve stress and keep the joy in being back to parenting.

When grandparents follow these suggestions to make being back to parenting a positive experience, they will feel less stress and more joy. They will use the resources God provides, allow others to be a part of their grandchildren's lives, and enrich the lives of their grandchildren in the process. They will be creative grandparents who love every minute of this God-appointed phase of their lives.

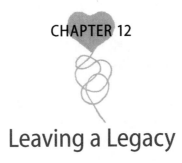

# CHAPTER 12

# Leaving a Legacy

One spinet piano, one grandfather clock, three lamps, two reclining chairs, one rocking chair, one stereo with assorted records including Lawrence Welk, Tennessee Ernie Ford, the Melody Four Quartet, and Doug Oldham. One jewelry box with no precious stones, silver, or gold. No oil paintings by the masters or priceless figurines.

My sister-in-law Jean and Judy were taking inventory of the items in Mom and Dad's house. Everything was exactly as they had left it when Dad experienced his emergency hospital admission. He then moved into a nursing home temporarily for rehabilitation and Mom moved into an assisted living facility.

On to the kitchen: three cast-iron skillets, four coffeepots, six cake pans, four pie plates. As we sorted through these items, I was overwhelmed with feelings of warmth. The kitchen was Mom's domain. She was a great baker; those pie plates held hundreds, maybe even thousands, of pies. Every week Mom would fill them with apples, pumpkin, or blueberries. Sunday after church, the family came for coffee. While the coffee was brewing, Mom would set out her latest creations.

It was a tradition, Sunday coffee at Mom and Dad's. We would laugh, talk, sip coffee, and enjoy the food and camaraderie. Coffee was poured into ironstone cups purchased from the grocery store when they were on special. Not china—often not matching. Worthless. But as memories flooded my mind, the cups and pie plates became priceless. We had memories that could never be broken, precious times that would never be stolen or sold.

My parents, Andrew and Edith, left a tremendous legacy of love to both their children and their grandchildren. Driving home from my father's funeral, I was pursued by a recurring question, "What memories will my children and grandchildren have of me? What will my legacy be?"

A *legacy* is the sum of what we leave to others, especially to our children and grandchildren. The writer of Proverbs reminds us that "a good man leaves an inheritance to his children's children" (Proverbs 13:22). To many people, legacy is all about leaving tangible possessions to friends and family members. But that is the least important legacy we can leave.

Many years ago one of my graduate professors assigned an exercise called "Heritage Trunk." As students, we had to make a list of tangible and intangible things we wished to transmit to our children and grandchildren. Some things we had already given to our children, others not. After compiling this list, we had to ask our children what tangible and intangible things they most wanted to receive from us. Then we were to ask our children what they had already received from us, especially the intangibles.

This was a moving experience for me and Judy. I remember our children telling me that I had given them a passion for life and a heart for serving others, and influenced their faith in God. It was gratifying to know that we had already given our children what matters most to us, the things that have eternal significance. I was reminded of Jesus' words, recorded by Matthew in his gospel:

> Do not store up for yourselves treasures on earth, where moth and rust destroy, and where thieves break in and steal. But store up for yourselves treasures in heaven, where moth and rust do not destroy and where thieves do not break in and steal. For where your treasure is, there your heart will be also. (Matthew 6:19–21 NIV)

My uncle Herm died many years ago after a lengthy bout with cancer. I didn't know him as well I as would have liked, but I enjoyed deer hunting with him for a few years before his death at the age of seventy-two. (I still remember his excitement when one of us would shoot a nice buck. One time he was so excited he gave a hunting buddy a kiss on the forehead!) My uncle's life had not been extraordinary, but his funeral was special. The service was focused on the Bible, and full of hope. A believer in Jesus Christ, my uncle had been ready to go from this life to the next.

During the funeral, members of his family shared memories of him. His five adult grandchildren each took a turn to speak. The youngest granddaughter stood last. As she spoke, her voice began to break and tears rolled down her cheeks. "My grandfather taught me many things," she said, "and I loved being with him on the farm. But I will always be grateful for what he told me about Jesus. His faith was real and powerful." She held her hand over her chest and said, "I will take his faith with me forever in my heart."

That young lady carries with her a legacy of faith from her grandfather. Even though my uncle was a man of modest means, he died with riches because his grandchildren love Jesus. As believing grandparents, our most important task is to leave a legacy by communicating and demonstrating our faith in Christ to our grandchildren.

## Communicating Faith

Communicating our faith to our grandchildren can be a daunting task. Grandchildren want to have fun with Grandpa and Grandma; they don't want to be lectured about God. Grandparents want to make their grandchildren laugh; they don't want to raise the somber issues of Christianity. Fortunately we don't need to lecture to communicate our faith. Instead we can demonstrate and communicate our faith by our character, conduct, and conversation.

### Our Character

One of the best ways to demonstrate our faith is by allowing God to produce in us the fruit of His Spirit: "The fruit of the Spirit is love, joy, peace, patience, kindness, goodness, faithfulness, gentleness and self-control" (Galatians 5:22–23 NIV). When our grandchildren see these characteristics in us, they see something to be desired—our character. I remember a granddaughter at an early age telling me how she helped another girl at school, how she listened and gave her advice.

After I commended her for her thoughtfulness, she said, "I'm just like you, Grandpa, helping others when they have problems." Today she is a lawyer in New York City, counseling others in the weighty matters of law.

I often wonder what aspects of my character I am leaving to my grandchildren. I wonder what they have already received from me. I hope they have seen in me and appropriated "love, joy, peace, patience, kindness, goodness, faithfulness, gentleness and self-control" as part of their lives.

## Our Conduct

The way we conduct our lives and relationships makes a strong impact upon grandchildren, who are always watching. They are influenced most positively when our conduct matches our words, especially regarding our faith. The Scriptures are clear on this matter:

> Do not merely listen to the word, and so deceive yourselves. Do what it says. Anyone who listens to the word but does not do what it says is like a man who looks at his face in a mirror and, after looking at himself, goes away and immediately forgets what he looks like. But the man who looks intently into the perfect law that gives freedom, and continues to do this, not forgetting what he has heard, but doing it—he will be blessed in what he does. (James 1:22–25 NIV)

Our grandchildren need to see our faith lived out in our daily lives. Godly, creative grandparents strive to do that, and thereby communicate their faith in a powerful way to watching, listening grandchildren. I have met many grandchildren who told me that their grandparent "lives his faith" and "practices what she preaches." I hope that is also true of me and you and other creative grandparents.

### Our Conversation

Grandparents tend to rely on their grandchildren *seeing* their faith, rather than *hearing* about their faith. Although seeing our faith is very positive and necessary for them, we know from Scripture that "faith comes from *hearing* the message" (Romans 10:17 NIV, emphasis added). Grandparents need to verbally share their faith with their grandchildren, as well as live out that faith in their presence.

Evidently many of us have decided that it is not our responsibility to verbally share our faith in Jesus with our grandchildren. We assume it is the parents' job. Primary responsibility for our grandchildren's spiritual education does fall on their parents, but that doesn't mean we may neglect to do our part. Some grandparents simply never talk to their grandchildren about faith. We may believe that it is important, and we may pray that our precious grandchildren receive Christ, but faith just "never comes up" in conversation.

A friend of ours, Marilyn, said it well, "The only thing we can take with us to heaven is the knowledge that our kids and our grandkids have accepted Christ and are going to be on the other side with us someday." My friend Perk said of himself and his wife, "It is our daily prayer that our children's children would have a personal relationship with the Lord, and that they would know the joy that's found in serving Jesus. We pray that the circle would not be broken, that we would all meet on the other shore someday."

Our grandchildren need to *hear* our story of faith, how we came to know the Savior. They need to hear us talk about what our faith means to us. Our daily lives should be sprinkled with stories about God meeting needs in our lives, stories about our need for God, and stories about service to God. If our faith is important to us and well integrated into our lives, sharing our faith freely will be easy. It will be natural to utilize teachable moments by telling stories of faith.

We cannot depend on character and conduct alone to communicate our faith. We all know good people who live well, but do not know Christ. We need to use words as well. We need to be clear in our verbal testimony of faith. When our lives match what our lips profess and our grandchildren see our faith in action, we leave them a godly legacy to emulate.

## A Godly Legacy

We leave a godly legacy when we live well, love well, serve well, and finish well.

### Live Well

We live well when we live without regrets. Regrets are actions that people wish they had taken or would do differently if given the chance. People have two types of regrets: what they have done and what they wish they had done. The latter of these two seems to be more important. People regret not doing what they later deem important.

Several years ago Judy and I did a study of regrets with over 1,400 people. The results were interesting and challenging. Look at the top ten regrets:

#1 regret:  I would live my life more in accordance with my religious principles.

#2 regret:  I would play more.

#3 regret:  I would be more lighthearted.
#4 regret:  I would do things that have value after I'm gone.
#5 regret:  I would spend more time with family.
#6 regret:  I would take more time to "smell the roses."
#7 regret:  I would laugh more.
#8 regret:  I would demonstrate more affection to family members.
#9 regret:  I would be more helpful to others.
#10 regret:  I would express appreciation more often.

Now read through the list again, this time considering whether you share these regrets. Then ask yourself, "Do my grandchildren see me living out my faith and values? Am I taking time to laugh and play with them? Do I spend time with them? Do they see me helping others and showing appreciation? Do they hear me say 'You did a great job' and 'thank you'?" Creative grandparents who want to live well will live without regrets. The Bible tells us, "Be very careful, then, how you live—not as unwise but as wise, making the most of every opportunity" (Ephesians 5:15–16 NIV).

Several years ago a friend of ours, Peter, talked to us about regrets. At the age of ninety-four, he said, "Regret is a waste, unless it brings change." We can't live our lives over, but we can live out the remaining days God gives us with gratitude and without regret. With God's help, we will

- Invest in things that have lasting value.
- Treasure relationships, and be more helpful and affectionate.
- Make wise choices and seize moments of opportunity.
- Express appreciation more often.

- Be more playful, light-hearted, and humorous.

This is living well.

### Love Well

We love well when we accept our grandchildren with their faults and foibles, loving them as they are, not only when they perform to our expectations. Judy often says, "We love our grandchildren unconditionally even in the times we do not approve of their behavior." She learned this lesson from her own grandmother.

When Judy was a teenager, she rebelled and did not want anything to do with faith. That is when I came into the picture. I rode up on my motorcycle in a black leather jacket, a high school dropout just out of jail for breaking and entering. She looked at me and actually thought, "That is Jerry Schreur, and I am going to show all those Christians that I am dating the bad boy of Hudsonville." And that is exactly what she did, except she not only dated me, she married me.

During those years, her Grandma Schut and her Aunt Lucille assured her they still loved her even though they were concerned about her lifestyle. When we visited her grandma, she was very kind to me and radiated the love of Christ. This same grandmother who would sit at the piano and sing the old hymns of faith with Judy when she was a little girl now lived out those songs. Judy knew she was loved even though they did not approve of her actions. She knew they were praying for her and also praying for me. The Lord honored those prayers.

### Serve Well

We serve well when we use our gifts, talents, time, and energy to benefit others. Most of us do a pretty good job of looking out for ourselves. I know I certainly do. Our natural tendency is to expend time and energy on things that benefit us. We pursue our careers, hobbies, and interests. While this is natural and necessary in moderation, it is God's desire for us to think more about serving others than ourselves. The apostle Paul, writing to the people at Philippi, said, "Do nothing out of selfish ambition or vain conceit, but in humility consider others better than yourselves. Each of you should look not only to your own interests, but also to the interests of others" (Philippians 2:3–4 NIV). Later in that same chapter, Paul reminds us that the Lord Jesus gave up the glories of heaven to come to this sin-cursed earth as a man, a servant, to die on a cross for us as the ultimate sacrifice. Our grandchildren need to observe people who serve well, people who unselfishly give of themselves to benefit others. Creative grandparents need to follow the example of Christ who "did not come to be served, but to serve, and to give his life as a ransom for many" (Matthew 20:28 NIV).

My friend Roger served well. Roger and I were both married students in Bible school. School always was easy for me, but not for Roger. He worked hard and still ended up with Cs for final grades. However, that did not discourage him. He faithfully studied and kept working hard. By his senior year, he was pastoring a small church in northern Michigan. He continued to serve that small group of people for nearly thirty years.

When people in Roger's small town needed a pastor for a wedding or a funeral, they called Roger. When they needed a counselor, they called Roger. When they needed someone to care for them in a crisis, they called Roger. He never wrote a book or published a journal article, and he was not given much recognition in this world, but in that small town he was their pastor. He was always there for them. Whenever I think of a faithful person, I think of my friend Roger. He was my hero!

Several years ago I received word of Roger's death. He had suffered a major heart attack. The townspeople mourned the loss of their pastor, a faithful servant of God. The last thing he did before he died was tell his grandchildren how much he loved them. Roger served well until the end.

### Finish Well

We start giving gifts to our grandchildren the day they are born. When Lauren, our first grandchild, was born, Judy took a twelve-hour bus trip to Michigan's Upper Peninsula to help take care of her for the first week. While Judy was gone, I went shopping. It was so much fun to buy little girl things. I spent more than I could afford on new baby clothes—dresses, short little bloomers, and sleeveless tops. Lauren might have been the best dressed baby in the Michigan Technological University student apartments. That was the beginning of my grandchild gift giving.

We continue giving gifts throughout their lives: Christmas, birthdays, graduations, special occasions, and just because we want to. Some of these gifts are remembered for a lifetime. As we all get older, the gifts change but still have meaning.

We don't know what the last tangible gift to our grandchildren will be, but we do know what our last gift will be. The final gift we give our children and grandchildren is showing them how to age gracefully and how to die. This can be quite a task but an important one. As Bette Davis said,

"Growing old is not for sissies." We will experience multiple changes and losses, both physical and emotional. Our grandchildren will watch us grow old. They will probably be there for us when we die.

One of the memories our sons Jack and Jon have of their Grandma Schreur is her grateful spirit. Even when she was bedridden the final six months of her life, she voiced her gratefulness to those who visited her and those who took care of her. She never complained and rather focused on the positive in her circumstances. When the grandchildren visited her, they went home with the blessing. Judy often mentions that my mother taught us all how to die gracefully.

We finish well when we live well, love well, and serve well until the end. As I contemplate my legacy, I want to be able to say with the apostle Paul, writing to Timothy, "I have fought the good fight, I have finished the race, I have kept the faith" (2 Timothy 4:7 NIV). I want to hear Jesus say, "Well done, good and faithful servant." That is the legacy of faith I desire to leave to my grandchildren.

What kind of legacy are you leaving to your grandchildren?

## Exercise: Heritage Trunk

Purchase a miniature trunk in which you include the following:

- A list of all the tangible things you wish to leave to your grandchild.
- A list of all the intangible things you wish to leave to your grandchild.

- A personal letter in which you describe positive characteristics you see in your grandchild.
- A letter in which you tell your grandchild how much he or she is loved.
- A letter in which you (once more) share your story of faith.

Give your grandchild the heritage trunk.

# Take the Challenge

Creative grandparents have a profound effect on their grandchildren. We may not realize our influence until they are adults, when we can see the principles they live by and the people they have become. Rest assured, though, that whatever the outcome, one of life's most rewarding experiences is grandparenting. This isn't just because of the results we see in our grandchildren, but because of what happens inside of us.

Creative grandparenting changes us. We become different people through our involvement with our grandchildren. We are shaped by our grandparenting experiences, even as we are attempting to shape our grandchildren. We are moved to tears of joy and frustration. We are never the same.

Creative grandparenting forces us to live the last third of our lives to the fullest, every single day. Involved grandparents become energetic and exciting people willing to try new things and take risks. Creative grandparents live with a profound sense of joy and purpose. Our grandchildren may not keep us from physically aging, but they do give us plenty of reason to get up in the morning and to treat each new day as a gift from God. An eighty-nine-year-old grandfather says that, after all these years, it is his relationship with his grandchildren that keeps him going. He loves to spend time with them, and they are frequent guests in his nursing home. Creative grandparents' lives overflow with love, and they are moved and changed by their encounters with their grandchildren.

Creative grandparenting is not just an act, and we can't fake it. It is a way of life, a conscious choice to throw caution to the wind and to dive into the lives of our grandchildren with reckless abandon. Our deepest desire is that the stories and suggestions in this book have filled you with the longing to make a difference in the lives of your grandchildren. Take the challenge.

This is your time to become a creative grandparent. Make a life-changing choice to become involved in your grandchildren's lives, for them and for you. Get started today. As our twenty-two-year-old granddaughter, Elena, told Judy, "You don't have to spend a lot of money on me, Grandma. Just be with me. Your presence is enough." Your presence means more than your presents. Be *with* them.

Your grandchildren will only be at this stage of life once. Now is the time to enjoy them and show them how much you to love and appreciate them. Enter their world, and invite them into your world. Allow creative grandparenting to change their life forever, and yours too!

# Note to the Reader

The publisher invites you to share your response to the message of this book by writing Discovery House Publishers, P.O. Box 3566, Grand Rapids, MI 49501, U.S.A. For information about other Discovery House books, music, videos, or DVDs, contact us at the same address or call 1-800-653-8333. Find us on the Internet at http://www.dhp.org/ or send e-mail to books@dhp.org.